T0195083

# WHAT REALLY HAPPENED
## IN THE
# GARDEN OF EDEN

ROBERT GLOVER

**author**HOUSE®

*AuthorHouse™*
*1663 Liberty Drive*
*Bloomington, IN 47403*
*www.authorhouse.com*
*Phone: 833-262-8899*

*Published by AuthorHouse   03/09/2022*

*ISBN: 978-1-6655-5116-8 (sc)*
*ISBN: 978-1-6655-5117-5 (hc)*
*ISBN: 978-1-6655-5118-2 (e)*

*Library of Congress Control Number: 2022902250*

*Print information available on the last page.*

## A FEW WORDS ABOUT THE AUTHOR OF:
## WHAT HAPPENED IN THE GARDEN OF EDEN

Praise the Lord every one my name is Robert Glover; I was born into this world on April 30, 1943 in the District of Columbia to my parents Benjamin Glover, and Mary Glover. I stayed with my parents from birth until five years old. At the age of five I moved to Amherst County, Virginia to stay with my grandparents, Robert Thomas Tinsley and Nannie Tinsley. I entered the Amherst County School System the age of six years old there I continued until graduation at the age of eighteen from Central High School, Amherst County, Virginia. Upon completing high school, I returned to the District of Columbia to live with my mother. I then was employed by the Morning Side dry cleaners as a presser, I worked at the dry cleaners for two years. In the year of 1964, I entered the United States Air Force, serving in several states, and overseas my last assignment was Vietnam, where I received an honorable discharge. Upon receiving my discharge, I returned to the the District of Columbia the month of April 1968 on the day of my return Dr. Martin Luther King Jr. was murdered, during that time there was a lot of soul searching with in me as to what would be my next move would be, I pondered what would be next for me. After two months I took the test for a position with the District of Columbia Police Department passed the test, and was sworn in two weeks later.

I worked for ten years, then I became a born-again Christian, and was Baptized into the *Holy Spirit* two years later, was called of *God* into the *Ministry of the Lord Jesus Christ.*

With the gift of teaching, I continued to work for the Police department until I retired in August 1988 still serving my *Lord and Savior Jesus Christ.* There is so much to learn of *Christ* no one person can do his will with out receiving from one another *Jesus* said, "Learn of Him" *Matthew 11:28-30, Matthew 28:18-20,* my prayer is that you will read this book with an open mind to receive more understanding of *God's* will for *His* children, *Jesus* being the family head may the blessing of the Lord continue to uphold you in all things, stay encouraged.

Sequence of events concerning Adam's fall in the garden of Eden GOD created Adam, in GOD'S image, and likeness <u>Gen. 1:26-28</u>. GOD also created two trees which depicts two family <u>lineages</u> one tree knowledge of good, and evil, one tree, tree of life. These two were set before Adam to choose Gen. 2:16-17 GOD told Adam that he could eat or partake of every tree freely, to eat means to think or desire of some by thoughts or thinking on a thing. <u>Prov. 23:7</u> to ponder a thought, then the thought will take form of what is thought on. Adam chose to eat of the tree that GOD commanded him not to eat, which is the law, Adam in spite of GOD's commandment, chose the law, now at that time Adam's spirit was not defiled, he was perfect, until he disobeyed GOD, then iniquity was found in him that's when sin entered into the world, and death by sin <u>Rom. 5:17-20</u> the law was not made for the righteous, that's when the law of sin, and death entered, and man became a slave to sin the law of sin and death entered into all mankind from that day on man's nature was sin. the attributes of the sin nature can be found in the law of Moses, that one is called a bottomless pitfull of as sin from Adam to Moses <u>Rom. 5:12-16</u> even over those who had not sinned according to Adam's transgression.

When Adam's offsprings were born which is the whole human race, sin nature was their inheritance, until one is born again that sin nature remain in all mankind, the law of Moses was given to show man to himself, man's nature. The law was condemnation of what was within mankind to

Adam's offsprings, the law was only to reveal to man GOD's displeasure with all mankind, Rom. 5:20, 2 Cor. 3:6-18 as Adam's offsprings try to do the law of Moses for righteousness they are rejected by GOD, because the sin nature cannot fulfil the law of righteousness. Therefore as one tries to do righteousness all that does is cause the offense to abound. All that is done is to add sin to sin, because the sin nature remains no removal of the sin, that is committed because the cause of the offense remains, because without faith it is impossible to please GOD. The law is not of faith, seeing that the free of the Knowledge of Good, and Evil is the law of the sinful nature, Adam's disobedience brought forth the sin nature of the law Adam is cursed forever, and cannot partake of the righteousness of the law of GOD's righteousness, the law of GOD's righteousness is against sinful Adam, sin is his nature, the law of GOD is the power

Of the sinful nature of Adam, so when Adam tries to justify himself by applying the law, he can only produce sin. Remember that everything produces after its own kind to sinful nature cannot produce righteousness of GOD's law. The power of GOD that brings forth more of the sinful nature is the law that was not made by GOD for the righteous man that GOD created in his own image, and likeness, Adam knew better, but he thought he could take the law, and use it for his own glory knowing good, and evil being self centered on himself not GOD. People cannot blame something outside of Adam the serpent mentioned is the earthly low nature of man animal like creature, in Adam's members, that fed his mind with lust of the flesh, lust of the eyes pride of life is not approved of GOD for his son. Every choice we make the effects of that choice is already predestined by GOD at creation everything no matter what, example the <u>moon</u>, <u>stars</u>, <u>sun</u>, <u>oceans</u>, <u>animals</u> these ail are in place and GOD need not speak to them again so it is with mankind, only difference is the man was given a choice, and every choice effect is predestined no matter what so we must be very careful of what we chose. The bible tells us what to think on

When Jesus was tempted as Adam was he had an answer for his soul, by way of the spirit which is pure, just as Adam, but Jesus was, and is not self-centered all glory to his father, there was not a being out side of Jesus tempting in Jesus mind, but he chose the tree of life, and reaped life everlasting praise GOD Jesus is our example of how to live according GOD's will. Remember as a man thinks in his heart so is HE. This has been since creation, and continues today. My prayer is that as you read you will accept GOD's word, and not fables of man pray that he remove these imaginations from us please, you will stop struggling with false doctrines of man. Learn as Christ, and chose life eternal. The law of sin in our members is GOD's power that reveals the sin nature not righteousness of GOD's law, man must be born again and have the nature of Christ to reveal the righteousness of the law that is our faith that please GOD know the TRUTH and be made free in Christ Jesus no one can please GOD, trying to do the righteousness of the law with the sin nature, we must abide

In Christ, and his word abide in us for the purpose of pleasing GOD our father. Thank GOD for the death of the sin nature that has given us access to grace, to partake of divine nature. Thank GOD for the cross of Jesus Christ, that justifies before GOD our father. Get rid of the old creation thoughts and desires that come to our mind daily, we are not a slave to its temptations because we have been, separated from the power of death by the death of Christ, sin does not rule because the sin nature is dead in all that belong to Christ Jesus our LORD.

Now we know that every choice we make, the energy is supplied by one power, and that power is the energy of GOD, no matter the choice tree of life or tree of the knowledge Good, and evil, so make sure we learn as Christ the tree of life, and live according to GOD's will for us. Eat with confidence that he's giving us good all the time. Having the spirit as Christ within guarantees us perfect peace. When Adam disobeyed GOD he received the curse of the law, and became a unrighteous man

That could not do the righteousness of GOD's law because of the cursed nature that he chose by his disobedience to GOD. I keep reminding us of this fact because it is very important, and is worth repeating over, and over thank GOD. Accept the simplicity of the gospel of Christ 2 Cor. 1:12. AMEN

# PART I

## INTRODUCTION

To what really happened in the Garden of Eden, and the effect it has on all humanity, from that time to now. Our LORD Jesus told us that we shall know the TRUTH, and His TRUTH shall make us free, that being the case, I have pondered in my mind why is there so much confusion in the world of believers in Christ. There are different denominations saying that they are the TRUTH, and all claim to be the body of Christ. If they are the body of Christ, why are there so many different teachings on Christ. The LORD put it on my heart to go back to the beginning in the book of Gen. 1:1 and I began to ask and seek, and knock, I could no longer fake man's word to be the answer, so I sought the TRUTH from the spirit of TRUTH, and got the answer, and peace of mind. As you read and, pray I pray that you receive the spirit of wisdom, and revelations in the knowledge of the LORD Jesus Christ. Only GOD knows his TRUTH, and he reveals himself to those that have the spirit of Christ his only be gotten son full of grace, and TRUTH. Now

# INTRODUCTION

**That GOD our Father has given us access to grace, and TRUTH. Let us draw near to him, with the full assurance of faith. The scriptures state that the natural man cannot know GOD's TRUTH, Jesus has revealed him in us by the spirit of GOD in the Holy Ghost 1 Cor. 2:9-14. We cannot allow ourselves to be under enticing words of man's wisdom. 1 Cor. 2:1-5 here are some fables that are not of the wisdom of GOD that tells us what happened to Adam in the Garden of Eden.**

1. Fallen angel from heaven

2. Apple eaten

3. Sex between Adam, and Eve out of season

4. A snake on the ground.

All of these are false No TRUTH. That is why I sought the LORD, and He heard my cry, thank you father GOD in the name of Jesus. Brothers, and sisters GOD will not have us to be ignorant of him. Let us read with our New Born Spirit, and not the letter of the Natural Intellect. May you receive your blessing of GOD's peace.

# PART I

In the beginning GOD created the heavens, and earth Gen. 1:1

What happened in the Garden of Eden, and its effect upon the whole human race? GOD said let us make man after our image, and likeness. GOD created Adam, and Adam was to be a son unto GOD with the attributes of God in his Spirit as a son who obeys his father, according to the commandments given by his Father. Gen. 1:31, GOD looked out on what he had created, and said it was good, and very good, no corruption at all, that gave him joy.

Adam was formed from the dust of the earth physically, then GOD breathed into the man Adam, and Adam became a living soul, the breath of life was the spirit of Adam received from the LORD, undefiled life when that life was received Adam became a living soul, with the ability to comprehend, with his soul, his will, emotion, and intellect as his spirit being the pre-eminence, where TRUTH is receive from GOD, with the soul, used to express GOD's will to his spirit. The soul is subjected to the spirit of GOD's expression of GOD's will. GOD never intended for man's soul to be the life principle in man, man's soul left alone as the life principal lives by sense observation, the five physical senses, according the

Impulsive movements in the body members, when GOD created Adam he created him to be a spiritual human being, led by revelation given to him by God Adam's spiritual faculties were to rule his soul, and body by inspiration given to his spirit from GOD. Adam's spiritual faculties were made up of <u>INTITUTION</u> which means the place where GOD's will is to be received, then his ability to commune with God, then his ability to know and bear witness to GOD's will called conscience, this is GOD's order for man to dwell with GOD in the spirit. The spiritual faculties are the most noble part of man, and it must be kept free to dwell with GOD in TRUTH.

What happened when Adam failed to follow GOD according to GOD's plan for mankind to dwell with Him? First of all GOD gave Adam the ability to choose what GOD had set before Him, GOD set before Adam two choices. <u>Tree of Life</u>, and the <u>Tree of the Knowledge of Good</u>, <u>and evil</u>. We must keep in mind that GOD controls, and has all power, regardless of appearance. Gen. 2:15-17 GOD told Adam what to expect of what he chose, the consequence of his choice was set before Him, but it was left up to him to choose, because GOD had given him free will, keep in mind GOD created these two trees

When GOD created the two trees he created <u>TWO</u> family lineages that Adam was to chose from for man to dwell upon the earth that would make up the human race, GOD gave the choice to Adam, remember that Adam has named all the beast of the field, every fowl of the air, and all was to reproduce after its kind Gen. 1:24-25. Gen. 2:18-20. We see from the scriptures that Adam was the spiritual Head of the Earth. Adam had authority from GOD to determine man's destiny on the earth. Keep in mind that every <u>creature</u> was reproduced after its kind. The choices that were given to Adam were within Adam, not some separate being outside of Adam, one nature was death, one nature was life eternal, one righteous, and one sinful represents what GOD set before Adam.

What was Adam's choice, and what was its effect on the whole human race. The choice that Adam made was the Tree of the Knowledge of Good, and evil. This choice is the knowledge of sin's nature Rom. 3:20. we see that this tree of the knowledge of good and evil is the law the scriptures states that the law is not for a righteous man, but the man that is of the law shall live by the law, Rom. 3:19.

When Adam chose the law, he separated himself from GOD's righteousness, and became a lawless creature by way of his disobedience. In <u>Gen. 2:17</u>, the law was not made for the righteous I Tim. 1:9-10, by Adam's disobedience he became what the law is against the sin nature the sin nature is now the Nature of Adam, and all of his offsprings the sin nature is the curse of GOD on Adam because GOD's commandment was disobeyed by Adam that made all mankind transgressors before GOD. There was nothing outside of Adam that caused him to be judged of GOD to be unrighteous <u>Rom. 5:17-21</u>

5

there was not a separate <u>entity</u>, we must honour GOD with our understanding of GOD's absolute <u>sovereignty</u>.

There is no other power; nothing has power, only GOD almighty. The question is asked what about the serpent that was spoken of in Gen. 3:1-5. The serpent mentioned is the lawless nature which is not for the righteous, the <u>serpent</u> is given because one who is under the law cannot think or walk in the strait Gate. His thinking is crooked, because His thinking is of self, and not GOD. The law focuses on man's self not GOD's righteousness of faith, causing man to be unjust in the sight of GOD. As we see with the eyes the LORD has given us to see we can know, as GOD would have us to know, the beginning of creation concerning man's relationship, and fellowship with GOD. Adam was created in GOD's image, and likeness, in the righteousness, as we know now Adam failed. Adam brought forth the law of sin and death <u>Rom. 8:1-3</u> when he yielded to the law in our members, Rom. 7:23 the law in our members, operate on sense observation of the five physical senses. Called the world this world was is in the mind of man's soul <u>intellect</u>, <u>will</u>, <u>emotion</u>. This is not acceptable with GOD <u>ZECHARIAH 4:6</u> only the spirit of GOD within us can please GOD, sisters, and brothers. Let us put away from us the <u>fables</u> that has been handed down from one generation to another, we must seek answers from GOD, he will help us <u>1 John 2:20-27</u> ask GOD for answers, instead of man's guessing games. The key to understanding GOD's will is to respect GOD's absolute sovereignty over all that he created every ounce of this universe is under his control. Nothing else I have heard so many fables about what happened in the Garden of Eden. There was no insurrection in heaven, no snake on the ground, no apple on the ground, no sex out of season

All of these fables have deceived serious minded people that desire to be close to GOD and transformed by the renewing of man's mind.

The LORD set before Adam life and death before life and death before Adam Gen. 2:17 Deut. 30:19 life, and death was within Adam to chose nothing outside of the man GOD created, for his Glory when Adam being a righteous man in perfect harmony with GOD chose to separate himself unto his earth. Thinking and brought sin and suffering upon all mankind, keep in mind that Adam had named the creatures of the earth, and creatures of the air, and GOD allowed it to stand, now when it came to man Adam chose death, and GOD allowed it but Adam was cursed, and could not access the Tree of Life because without faith it is impossible to please GOD Gen. 3:22-24 Remember nothing outside of man can harm man Mark 7:14-23 No food no being is the cause it's within man's sin nature Jere. 17:9 When Adam sinned he exercised his choice to do what he did with that choice came effects of that choice. When Adam made his choice to live according to the law the consequences of his choice was already in place or predestined by GOD in his work of creation Is. 45:5-7, When Adam made His choice HE inherited the law of sin and death, the law of sin and death came by the man Adam Rom. 5:17-21, We should make special attention to this fact, because some will blame GOD, but GOD cannot be blamed for sin, because GOD does not impute sin and unrighteousness into mankind, true He created all but for Himself. Prov. 16:4 He warned Adam not to partake of the Tree of Knowledge of Good and Evil (which is the law) for those that oppose GOD's commands. When Adam disobey GOD he became a law breaker, and was cursed, and his seed after him. The law of sin and death came by Adam, the Law of Moses was given to Adam's off springs to show them the unrighteous condition of their heart, the Law of Moses could not deliver them from the sin nature only to show them their transgressions, until the spirit of Christ would come. The law's power is GOD 1 Con. 15:56. The sin nature's effects are powered by GOD's law. Here is its operation man in His sinful nature knows right from wrong according to his own understanding mainly for self preservation, self glory all about self not GOD. When this person is told of the law of Moses, he tries to do what the law says, but cannot, why because of the sin nature the command is not compatible with the sin nature, these two are oppose to one another, and cannot achieve its desire for righteousness of the law sinful man, man's sinful nature

Man cannot walk according to GOD's grace, because these two do not agree Amos 3:3, the more a unrighteous person try to do the deeds of the law all that does is to increase the effects of the sin nature, deliverance is not present Rom. 5:20

the law in the sin nature causes the power of sin to abound, what causes it to abound the <u>law</u> 1 Con. 15:56 like I said before GOD is the power behind all that happens no matter what it is, it's all of GOD, it was predestined when he creates the world. Every man born into the world has an awareness of right, and wrong but how to perform righteousness is cut off for the reasons mentioned here first when Adam sinned he lost his ability to communicate with GOD in his spirit he lost his institutive ability to receive GOD's will in his spirit, this is apart from the soul's observations of the senses, 5 physically, second he lost his ability to worship GOD in spirit, and TRUTH to reverence GOD, honour GOD, praise GOD in His spirit that ability is called communion these two abilities Adam lost completely death came. Now the third ability of Adam was conscience now this is the only part of Adam that remained with him after he sinned, he was left with the ability to know some form of right, and wrong

The conscience even in its unrighteousness has kept man from totally destroying each other; this fall of Adam places man in the category of <u>Animals</u> man has no pre-eminence over a beast <u>Ecc. 3:16-21</u> GOD cannot accept man's conscience because it's of the earthly nature where sin rules man. Please do not blame GOD for our failures <u>James 1:13-18</u> GOD does not impute unrighteousness Rom. 4:18, Rom. 32:2. To those that will say, that GOD is in it so it must be <u>ok</u>, but like I said before GOD is in everything because he created all things, but the difference is that what is the will of GOD we must seek GOD as true believer to know His will, remember that we are to serve His purpose, we see all manner of lawlessness committed every day, and we complain, make new laws, punish the lawless, but no peace because the sin nature cannot remove the cause, and effect of man's discomfort, because only GOD in Christ can remove the cause, and effect of man's discomfort Acts 4:12, we need the new nature, 2 Con. 5:17 mankind does not respect GOD, churches are still preaching, and teaching according to Moses law. Do's and don'ts of the law

Go instituted the new testament church to impute righteousness to all that would believe in the death burial and resurrection of Jesus Christ as our justification before Him Rom. 10:9-10 Acts 2:38-39 Mark 16:15-18. GOD laid the foundation for to build people in to himself Is. 46:13, Is. 51:15 Is. 56:1, Rom. 1:17, Is. 54:17 Rom. 4:13 1 Cor. 1:30, 2 Cor. 5:21 Rom. 5:17 Rom. 4:5 Phil. 3:9 Eph. 2:20 according to these scriptures, and these are many, many more that show GOD will for man to be righteous. The church for the most part is bound up with being perfected in the flesh. Instead of pointing man away from the thing called self, unto Christ our life in epistles. We see man trying to perfect himself by the deeds of the law. Gal. 3:15-21 if we preach, and teach, and above all live Christ we would be better witnesses of Christ, instead of self righteousness, we have to know Jesus Christ spirit with in every believer John 5:39-47 Jesus warned us just reading the law is not sufficient we need the spirit, because in the spirit the righteousness of the law is fulfilled Matt. 5:17

Trying to be transformed by just reading the bible, and praying is not enough, quoting scriptures is not enough, and just attending church service is not enough. We need to know GOD by our spirit of Christ which is in every believer; we must get to know him Job. 22:21 we must know Him within us not by outward appearance of man's customs, and standards. In the book of Col. 2:8-23 A lot of these customs, and standards are of some that would glory in appearance rather than pure heart 2 Con. 5:12-13 Lam. 3:21-33 Gal. 6:11-18, Matt 23:1-12. There are many born again people that would look at me with dismay if I said that you have the spirit of Christ, your spirit has been made alive in Christ Eph. 2:1-10, now that we are alive with the spirit of Christ being our life we are now build upon Christ Eph. 2:20-22, we are no longer bound but free Rom. 8:1-3 we as ministers of Jesus making us sons with the seed of his only begotten we have the measure that is sufficient to keep us before the father, now that we are sons having the same spirit of faith 2 Con. 4:13 we come to GOD our father the only qualifications is to have the nature of Christ, he has accepted us in His beloved son in whom he is well pleased now Jesus is not praying for us nor are we praying to Him, we are sons of the son, having access now that the cursed. Nature the old nature is dead, put on the new man Eph. 4:22-24 we must keep in mind that we have the spirit of Christ within us;

I know some people even souls that have been saved for many years will have trouble with what I am writing

GOD wants us to focus on Him now that we are His family. We must think, and speak words from our spirit words that GOD will impute to hearers GOD cannot impute words of condemnation we must know the voice of the Holy Ghost within our reborn spirit no longer bound think on these things Phil. 4:8-9 Col. 4:5-6 in the Book of Acts the Apostles preached Jesus, not the law of Moses, and we see the results of their labour, we must continue to carry on what was started in the book of acts, Jesus referred to the law of Moses in the Four Gospels as your law John 8:17, John 15:26 we see that the law of Moses was given to Adam's off springs not the the new creatures in Christ 2 Cor. 5:17 the law applied to man's self not GOD's righteousness of the law. We need the mind of Christ John 5:30 John 8:28-29, we must keep our spirits and souls dedicated to GOD, for reconciliation to take place, be filled with the spirit 2 Cor. 5:20. Again we must know without a doubt that whatever choice we make, the effect of our choice has already been established by GOD our creator, whatever it is. Chose life Jesus is the Tree of Life. Adam's Tree is Death, learn of Christ

GOD will not, and cannot impute the law of Moses for righteousness, Rom. 8:5-8 the law of the righteousness of faith must done in the new nature in Christ Jesus image only, acts 4:12 the more the law Moses is spoken to the canal man, the more sin manifested with in mankind even in the life of one who is born again, this same principle applies Gal. 2:15-21, Gal. 3:1-14. If GOD imputed the law of Moses to mankind for salvation then we would live in corruption forever Gen. 3:24 GOD in his mercy showed compassion by not allowing man to live in a corrupt nature forever, for by the law of Moses is the knowledge of sin does not lead to perfection, it only shows man it is inheritance from the first Adam, the law showed man that he needs to be born again in Christ Jesus John 5:39-47 Luke 24:44. It is a very sad situation when that are in position to lead souls to Christ, are drawing people to themselves that is against GOD's will men have made them a <u>cult</u> instead of the body of Christ, many call themselves the body of Christ, but in works they deny the LORD, Jesus warned us to be careful when they say the Christ is here or there Matt. 24:23-26

When Adam sinned in the garden of Eden the consequences or effect of his choice was already in place long before it happened, just if one was told not to touch a live electric wire, and he refuse to listen, and touch it in spite of the warning he will suffer for his action, that wire did not just become alive when he touched it, no it was already live before it was touched, when we sin the consequences of our choice is a live wire, so to speak the consequences were predestined long before I made the choice, so it is with every action we take righteous or unrighteous we must take caution to know GOD's will before engaging in any action, because our life is at stake, Matt 7:21-27 Matt 7:13-14.

## What about the
## Devil

I do not give time to talking about the devil as man perceives the devil. The devil is describes as one opposed to GOD's righteous commands, really as man perceives the devil is rooted in the imagination of man's mind, because man's perception of the devil is to perceive something having power, but that cannot be TRUE, because GOD has all power, and there is no other

Christ must receive in our spirit the word of reconciliation for GOD's converts 2 Cor. 5:17-21, we are to put in the time, and effort to prepare to truly minister to GOD's justified souls in Christ Jesus.

Converts need to be assured that GOD has taken them to be His own he is our blessed assurance the he is our Father no condemnation 2 Cor. 3-1-18, please read these scriptures take the time it is important very important.

# Having the Name
# of Jesus

The scriptures tells to look to Jesus Heb. 12:1-3, John 5:39-47 there are many scriptures that tell us to always look to Jesus, and desire him, his nature, to look to Jesus is to abide in his nature John 15:1-7, we are told to acknowledge every good thing in us, our new nature. In Christ Jesus Philemon verse six, my soul must always acknowledge that I am a new creation in Christ, therefore it is all good no corruption 1 Pet 11:22-23 what is important is the seed which is Christ Gal. 3:14 the promise not seeds but one Christ Gal. 3:16 Col. 1:27 Christ with in 1 John 4:4 as we read we see that the spirit of Christ the seed that GOD has given us is pure no darkness at all, Col. 3:1-8 in the Book of Hebrews 1:1-14 there in the old testament. God.

GOD spoke to his people by the prophets, what did he speak, He spoke by the law of Moses condemnation 2 Con. 3:6-18, Gal. 3:13-14, with the law of Moses is the knowledge of sin the law could not make man perfect Heb. 9:9-10, man's conscience could not bear witness to GOD's righteousness because man was dead spiritually now in Christ our spirit is made alive by the death of our Lord Jesus Christ Eph. 2:1-2 now we have access to grace by faith Rom. 5:1-5. Having the incorruptible seed which is the nature of Christ Jesus 1 Pet. 3:4. Now that we are justified in Christ we have GOD himself to be our father Gal. 4:6, <u>Rom. 8:14-17</u>, <u>Heb. 10:22 Is. 32:17</u> we now live on the effects of our righteousness <u>1 Cor. 1:30</u>

# Praying in Jesus
# Name

One thing I have noticed in John chapter 16, Jesus made a statement about approaching the father, after he was to be glorified <u>John 7:37-39</u> now looking into John 16:1-28 here Jesus is talking with His disciples about the glory that is to be revealed upon his death, burial and resurrection, and he told

Them something that I never hear any one mention I received the Baptism of the Holy Spirit in the tear of 1981, and heard many things taught but this is one thing I haven't heard, but in Jn 16:7-16, he's telling them what to expect when they receive his nature, and is baptized in the Holy Ghost, he goes on to tell them about the rejoicing that would follow after his resurrection. In verse 23 John 16:23 in that day you will ask Him nothing, but having his nature or name we could ask the father, and the father would give it to us. John 16:24 he says up until now you have ask nothing of the father, having his nature, but when that day come your joy may be full, he spoke to them in Proverbs, in earthly language to explain a spiritual TRUTH, but when they will receive his nature they will know the Father plainly, when in John 16:26 when his incorruptible seed 1 Pet 1:22-23 there would be no need for Him to pray to the father on their behalf. John 16:27 having Lord Jesus, and believe, he came out from GOD we can approach GOD as sons of GOD joint heirs with Christ joint heirs with his nature his attributes Rom. 8:14-17, His adoption of us is not the adoption of mankind, man's

Man's adoption is based on legal requirements of man's law, but what separates man's adoption from GOD's way of adoption is the seed, man can adopt a child but that child's seed belongs to another man, because that man's attributes cannot be demonstrated in what he has adopted, but GOD's adoptions is different, because the cross of Jesus made it possible for GOD to put the seed of his son into us

There is no other separate entity apart from GOD, to say that there is something that has power, other that GOD is far from the TRUTH, to think that there's a separate entity from GOD with power to contend with GOD is fruitless, when GOD spoke in <u>Gen. 6:3</u> he noted that man's attributes were flesh, no power, the flesh has no power, <u>Heb. 2:6</u>, <u>Ro. 8:3-4</u> the fleshly attributes of man Is. 2:22, <u>Ps. 144:4 Ps 39:5</u>, we see in scriptures that all discords, and inharmony between GOD, and man is the sin nature of man nothing else the carnal man is no match for GOD, and Jesus within us, all carnal man does is serve the law, the only way to do the righteousness of the law is that the carnal man must die, because the law is of GOD, and will never cease, nor can owe ignore the law, otherwise apart from death of the old nature in man, man will never have peace for the law is Holy, <u>Rom. 7:12-25</u>, until one dies he will be undecondemnation, because GOD does not honour man's sin nature upon being born again then the righteousness of the law is fulfilled Matt. 5:17-20. 1 Cor. 10:11-15, James 1:13-18 MARK 7:14-23, when the man Jesus was tempted forty days, and forty nights the bible said he was tempted of the Devil, he was tempted to follow the law of sin in his members, just as the first Adam Rom. 7:23 thoughts were going to his mind, there was no being external to himself tempting him it was the carnal nature trying to get him to submit to its will Jesus being our example, we must know, and follow in his footsteps. We are able to walk in his way acts 1:8. Knowledge is very important we cannot allow ourselves to be destroyed for lack of knowledge Hosea 4:6 we must not beat the air 1 Cor. 9:26-27 beating the air is effort without any substance, no spiritual growth.

Now that we are Dead Rom. 6:1
To the old nature
What now

Believer are now free from the bondage of the old creation death, now what is next, the scriptures say that we are now to be transformed by the renewing of the mind Rom. 12:1-3, put off the old man Eph. 4:22 now that we are born again, we are still in the presence of the sin nature but not controlled by its ways, we now are controlled by the new nature which is Christ Jesus we were born again in the spirit, made alive with Christ nature, now our spirit is pure incorruptible 1 Pet. 1:22-25.

The incorruptible seed is Christ, but now we have the responsibility to renew our minds to conform to the new spirit when we were born again in spirit our soul was not totally, there were something with the soul that was removed, but there are still some of the old creations ways that are still there, some more stronger than others, before we were born again we were one lump of sinful flesh nature, spirit, soul, and body now that we are born again in spirit we now have the ability to bring the soul in compatible, our souls need to be purified all that is of the old creation must be removed, by the daily washing of GOD's word in the spirit, daily we need for GOD's spirit in the Holy Ghost to quicken our spirit which in turn helps to possess our soul in the righteousness of faith, GOD acts directly upon our spirits, then the soul must conform to the incorruptible seed our new spirit 1 Pet. 3:4 then the soul, and body. We are to proclaim the LORD's death daily Luke 9:23, 1 Cor, 11:23-34, Eph. 5:26 the soul needs a daily washing not just reading the bible only on praying or quoting scripture but it has to be the Holy Spirit revealing GOD's purpose into our spirit intitutively then our conscience bears witness to GOD's will whatever he reveals to the spirit.

We must always remember that we are his workmanship and not our own Eph. 2:10 we are to serve His purpose not man Eph. 1:6, 9-11 we are vessels made by GOD to honour Him according to His purpose, he does not need man's wisdom we need to seek him for Him. Most of man's seeking GOD is for man's self interests and not GOD's will, we should always seek GOD's will, because GOD's will is good toward mankind always good not evil. <u>Jere. 29:11</u> the soul of mankind left alone will quench the spirit the soul needs to be subject to the spirit of TRUTH with in man's new spirit let us follow GOD's order first the spirit, soul, body we are clothed from within, in contact with GOD's spirit within our newly created spirit. The animals are clothes from outside, because we are in GOD's image we are set apart from all creation let us rejoice at how much he cares for us to live his life within us praise his Holy name, our affection must be set on Christ, and his desires not the observation of the soul Luke 17:20-21 if we walk according to the soul's observation, we make ourselves a friend of the world because the senses receives it's impulses from the law of sin in the body members that's why we are fed life from within.

I pray as you read this book you will read it with the desire to know our GOD, a father, I pray that you will seek the LORD's will and be willing to conform to his TRUTH which brings forth his peace to dwell within our spirit soul, and body 1 Thess 5:23 there are so many voices in the world today but we must seek the voice that will deliver us from all vanity of Man's Wisdom. All Glory belongs to GOD, and I am blessed that he has used me to bear witness to his TRUTH, thank you Father GOD for this privilege to publish you name thanks Deut 32:3-4 May GOD bless you all forever, love you.

# PART II

➤ Our conscience is responsible to God.

God is Judge.    I Corinthians 8:4

Romans 14
Function of Conscience

Deuteronomy 2:30 – Harden spirit
Psalms 34:18 – Crushed in spirit, contrite
Psalms 51:10 – Right spirit
John 13:21 – Troubled spirit
Acts 17:16 – Saw
Romans 8:16 – Bear witness
I Corinthians 5:3 – Pronounced judge
II Corinthians 2:3 – Rest, no rest
II Timothy 1:7 – Timidity, not spirit of fear
John 8:9 – Convict
Romans 9:1 – Witness
I John 2:20 – Unction

Effect Change
Hebrews 9:9
Hebrews 9:14
Hebrews 10:2
Hebrews 10:22
I Peter 3:21

I Corinthians 8:7

Conscience follows

Give confidence by revelation
Institution knowing
Conscience – spiritual organ

*Internal or self-knowledge of right and wrong according to God's will, not human reasoning. Conscience never argues or reasons. It discerns by way of intuition knowledge. God's children should not by human reasoning. Conscience speaks for God's will, not reason. Man can justify himself by reasoning but man's explanation does not please God. God's conscience demands our obedience.

* Acts 23:1, Acts 24:16

Conscience is limited by knowledge.

Romans 7:7 If we are not aware of an offence, his conscience does not affect his fellowship with God. Our conscience is only able to abide in the light that we have. A good conscience assures us that as far our knowledge goes, we are prefect; have arrived at the goal at hand, but not the ultimate goal. We are renewed daily to reach that goal, due to different stages of growth.

II Corinthians 10:5, I John 3:18-24

Even with much knowledge, we still need to be spirit led, as how to use knowledge. = Wisdom

➤ Still small voice.

Perfect perception, given by God.

12/23/2020 Bible Study

Intuition – I John 2:20

Intuition is a part of our spiritual faculty that has been quicken in the new birth. Which is given for us to know the things of God. I Corinthians 2:9-15

We know by our spirit. We understand with the mind. The Holy Spirit enables our spirit to know the things of God. Then our spirit instructs our mind to understand what the Holy Spirit had revealed in the spirit of man.

New man – Romans 8:14

To perceive correctly – Mark 2:8-10

Reasoning is of observation of the soul. *It's subject to error.

God reveals himself by revelation.

Matthew 16:13-19, John 3:1-11, Matthew 26:41, Mark 8:12, Colossians 1:8

Love is a spirit.

Ephesians 1:17, I Corinthians 14:16, John 13:21, John 11:33, John 4:23, John 16:14

## Spiritual Healing

I must rise above the carnal concepts of <u>good and evil</u>. The mind must be an instrument of receptivity of the revelation revealed in the spirit to the mind. Spiritual truth assimilated in my spirit, becomes part of my mind and body. The spirit is principal. Our senses testify erroneously. This world is not an illusory. But man's concept of the world is an illusion. I need the increase of awareness. In order to realize the all power of God, man's concepts of the material world must be denied. Renew my mind.

Sin and sickness is unreal in God's Kingdom.

## Tree of Knowledge of Good and Evil

All power is to have power over all of Adam's false precepts. Concepts = that which exists in the mind as thoughts. In the mind, not based on the spirit's revelation of the Holy Spirit in man's spirit.

Hebrews 11:1-3

Substance = Reality behind the Form substance is spiritual, that brings forth the Form.

There are two tress in our garden, but only <u>one power, that power is spiritual</u>. One is spiritual; spiritual because it is the spirit that is manifested, as <u>Form</u>. The <u>one</u> world, which is material sense imagination, conceived in the mind of mankind. The human concept of power is to conquer power to things, conditions, places, situations, sickness and health. The acknowledgement of <u>power</u> of mind and matter; then part of the time accepting God as the Great power over the power of mind and matter. The church must lift itself above the imagination of power of mind and matter.

Examples:

1. Moses and Pharaoh
2. Elijah over the <u>non-power</u> of his <u>persecutions</u>. Jesus provided the <u>non-power of lack</u>, <u>limitations</u>, <u>sin</u>, <u>disease and death.</u> The word of truth, which comes by revelation of the spirit within. Then comes freedom. Romans 8:1-3 Free now that grace operates in my <u>spirit and soul</u>. I must develop my <u>spiritual faculties</u> to dwell in truth.

In the human world of imagination, there is only one universal mind that receives <u>impulses</u> of both good and evil, common to all mankind. This universal mind is made up of pairs of <u>opposites</u>.

Examples:

1. Health – Sickness
2. Life Death
3. Wealth – Poverty
4. Good - Evil

The temptations we face is the same <u>Jesus</u> faced. To <u>judge</u> or be <u>judged</u> by material sense, I have to know God to be myself hood. In order to overcome, abide in the life principal of Christ Jesus. Genesis 1:31

We cannot carry out anything physically without accepting it in the <u>mind</u>. The world is of mind. It is in the material sense of God's spiritual world. II Corinthians 10:4-7

I need to experience less of the effects of the carnal mind of man and more of the fruit, of the mind of Christ. The material sense of existence is responsible for the discomforts in mankind, no devil to blame. Do not allow material sense to deceive me. I must guard my heart and soul, not to conceive material sense. Remember god is spirit. Genesis 1:1, In the beginning God created. God is spirit. What man calls second creation, is an <u>illusory</u> creation of the <u>five senses</u>. Physical sense - imaginations, but there is no unreal or <u>illusory</u> world. But there is a sense of the unreal. Material sense builds the human identity, then be anxious for its life, health, supply, home and companionship. Does not realize that God - spirit, is all.

Genesis 1:31

Material sense <u>imprisons</u> the mind of man. I need spiritual <u>perception</u> to be witness to God's wisdom. Depending on the five physical sense will give a false <u>testimony</u>. Help me to hear your still small voice in my spirit. Possess my soul. Exercise patience in my spirit by the Holy Ghost. Possess my soul.

Luke 21:19

The Spirit of God is the substance, cause and law of all creation. Always be a witness behind the appearances. Know the truth - God's spirit bear witness with my spirit. Call no human <u>good or evil</u>. I expect God to reveal in my spirit; God's truth, which is spirit. God is manifested as my individual being. The way to get rid of the fleshly man is to realize God as my individual.

Galatians 2:20-21

II Corinthians 5:17 In Christ Jesus the Holy Ghost removes the personal sense of "I". Do no try to get God's grace to operate in the personal sense of existence. Do not attempt to benefit the natural man with the grace of God. Matthew 6:25-33

Everything starts and ends with God, which is our completeness in Christ.

Hebrews 12:1-3, Habakkuk 2:20, Psalms 46:10

There are two family lineages within our garden. Luke 6:43, Hebrews 4:12

These lineages must be separated by the spirit of God. Help me Father to bear witness to <u>truth</u>. The demonstration of the spirit of health, instead of the health of the material minded person, spirit the wonderful works of God. The contrast is Babel was focused man's works, at Pentecost the focus was on God's wonderful works. John 17:21 Unity in Christ Jesus is the only way to unity. Hebrews 11:1-3 Seek God in Christ then Unity will come. John 6:28-29 Jesus is the finished work of God. Jess is the only way. Colossians 1:28-29 God is looking for his son in us.

Hebrews 1:1-14, Acts 17:25 God is not served by man's hand, John 4:23-24. We are changed by the way we behold the Lord. II Corinthians 4:18 Behold Him in his glory not man. Behold him in his spirit, then we are formed into the same image, Matthew 26:64. I must know him in the power of his resurrection. Know him in his new nature, John 16:7. I cannot know him in natural sense perception. I must know him by revelation in my spirit helped by the Holy Ghost. John 14:9, Matthew 17:14, Matthews 17:1-8

Man must forget about what he can build and <u>Hear the Lord</u>!

➢ Rest in Christ

Hebrews 4:1, Hebrews 4:11, Deuteronomy 5

Out of <u>Egypt</u> into <u>Canaan</u>. Out of <u>Adam</u> into <u>Christ</u>. God brought us out of Egypt, (Adam). But we have to strive to be formed in Christ. Galatians 4:19 Christ must be formed in us. Canaan is a type of man's heart before redemption in <u>Christ Jesus</u>. The heart and soul must be free of the 'Ikes'. The soul must be filled with the promise of God, which is the spirit of Christ, the new man. In the wilderness of ups and downs; back and forth; repenting and going down again; there is no rest. One has to learn to trust God's spirit for the rest. Jesus gives us access to God's grace, which is our rest. Life in the wilderness is a life of want. In Canaan there is plenty. In the wilderness there is a life of lack of food and water. God gave them manna, but they were not content. It resulted in murmurings. But in Canaan there was a supply vineyards they had not planted. God was their need revealed. I thank God that in Christ we are saved from the darkness; to Jesus' grace, which is sufficient. In the wilderness there is no victory. But in the promise land, there was victory. As we enter into God's rest in Christ, we have Victory over the sin and self-life. Philippians 4:13, Romans 8:37 I must know that I have that life within. I ask you Father to help me live this life. I have not lived the life promised me in Christ. I ask for forgiveness and cleansing. I confess your spirit of mercy. I ask that you be glorified. I thank you for the life you live in me. Help me to give up all appearance of self, good and evil according to the tree of the knowledge of good and evil. Please help me to guard my heart. Provers 4:23 Abstain from the wisdom of the earthly thinking.

> ➤ Asking in faith is expecting the grace of God.

Faith of God within real faith requires patience. To have the faith of God, I must have a spiritual vision. I must seek to have the spirit of faith, which is of God - for his glory. I cannot focus on temporal things. Fleshly lust is grounded in fear and self-preservation. II Corinthians 4:18 I am asking God to open the eyes of my heart. Abraham's faith was of his spiritual vision, when he offered up his son Isaac. That vision was that God would sacrifice his only begotten son for the sin of the world, John 8:56; that is the true faith, to have the spirit's vision. Ephesians 1:18 True faith is knowing Jesus. I must trust in the word himself, not just reading and quoting scriptures. True faith comes by seeing the Lord and its fruit will be <u>love</u> and <u>humility</u>. Counterfeit faith will always be <u>pride</u>, feeding man's lust and not <u>his sprit</u>, earthly minded. Romans 8:5, I Timothy 6:6-12 To be rich or poor in the world's goods have nothing to do with our spirituality. Philippians 4:11-12 True faith is given by the lord so that we can be found in Him. II Corinthians 1:20 The promise is given to the seed, Christ. We knowing the seed, which is Christ. We are accepted in Him. Galatians 3:16 He is my inheritance Ephesians 1:18-19 God does not deal with mankind apart from the seed – Jesus nature. John 14:12 In the beginning years of being born again, we rejoice with the outer man's comfort. John 6 But as we grow or should grow, our motives will have to change. Jesus' spirit is now my life. I must be transformed according to the life He lives among us.

Galatians 4:1-6

When our motives are changed, we will learn to be content regardless of the outer world of our being because our hope is in the unseen. II Corinthians 4:16-18, Matthew 6:63

> ➤ Faith and Patience

Romans 10:9-10, Hebrews 6:12

True faith and patience go together. I must realize patience is faith in action. Romans 4:18-20

Time and space is of man. We must have the mind of Christ, which is not time and space. Manifestation of God's grace is determined by God, not man's time and space attitude. When Abraham believed God, the seed sowed in his heart; that was not the fruit. The seed had to be watered and cultivated to become a healthy plant to bear fruit. True faith is seeing God in everything. I must see him and abide in him.

John 15:1-7

Example of Joseph – Genesis 50:14-26

With what happen to him, some would say, he did not have enough faith; but God had him, where he wanted him and used him greatly. We must desire God so we can truly be partakers of his nature.

Psalms 115:1-2 All things are for Him, and by Him. I must be willing, always to glory His name. Colossians 1:16-18 When we lose patience, we bring forth corrupt fruit. Look at Abraham. He had a loss of patience and brought forth a child that was not of the promise. Then that which is corrupt, will punish that which is incorrupt, the promised seed.

➢ Looking for a city

Hebrews 11:10, John 6:29

Christ Jesus alone has to be our belief. Flesh of man cannot believe. I Peter 1:21 I must be single minded. James 1:1-12 There is only one foundation – Jesus. I Corinthians 3:11 There is only one message – Jesus.

Colossians 2:3 Really Jesus is the whole building. Ephesians 4:15 Help us to be in the mind set where Christ is formed in us, the work of the ministry. We must seek Jesus instead of doctrines and standards. Colossians 1:17 In him doctrine can be established. In Christ, is on whole loaf. Doctrines can lead to division, which can fragment the body, which is extremes of man. Hebrews 1:1-2

Hear Jesus – II Corinthians 3:8 Jesus is here to be truth in us. John 11:25 Jesus has to be the whole, so that grace can abound. Song of Solomon 1:7 - a type of the bride

The spirit of Jesus alone is the mediator between God and man. I Timothy 2:5 The ministry must never take Jesus' place, but to be a shepherd to the flock. No minister is to establish his own authority.

John 10:16 Jesus is the chief shepherd. All must be of His spirit.

Matthew 23:8-12

All spiritual labor is for Christ to be formed in his people. I must decrease! John the Baptist led John and Andrew to Jesus. John 1:36-42 Lead me to Jesus, not just church. Truth is not a system it is Jesus.

> ➤ Christ humility – My salvation     Philippians 2:5-8

Be humble! Deny self! Be willing to be a vessel, empty of pride. The door of my heart must be open unto the spirit. Revelation 3:20 I must take the low place. Pride is the one thing that hinders me. Self-will has to go. My knowledge of right and wrong must be denied; that is of the tree of knowledge of good and evil.

When Adam sinned, he was brought captive to sin. II Corinthians 4:4 The god of this world is carnal nature – Adam; controlled by the law of sin and death. Romans 8:3 I, I Corinthians 15:56-57

The law is the power by which carnal man lives. Romans 5:12, Romans7:8-11

Flesh – man's personality – is controlled by sin, and directed by selfish ambitions; rather than service to God. Romans 8:2 The law of the spirit of life, working by the holy spirit in the new man; is not mechanical, but life. The law of sin and death is a power. Carnal man is the servant of sin. Romans 7:23

The carnal self is put to death by the cross of Christ, which separated man from sin's power.

I Corinthians 15:56-57 Now that I am dead, the law of sin does not have dominion over me. The law did not die on the cross, but now the new creature life has fulfilled the Law of Moses. Matthew 5:17

The nature that Moses' Law addressed is dead. The Law of Moses is fulfilled in Jesus' righteousness.

I Corinthians 1:30 Now wisdom is building God's house in Christ Jesus. Hebrews 3 &4, I Peter 1

The spiritual house is based on spiritual promises. If grace is to abound, I must submit to Gods' self, and be his servant. I Peter 5:7-8

> ➤ The do nots of the law, do not apply to Christ. Colossians 1:27, Colossians 5:17

Romans 3:30-31 Thank God for access to the tree of life, in Christ. Thank God for the new spirit.

Spirit Image of Christ

- Eyes
- Ears
- Knowing

Spirit's function

- Institution
- Communion
- Conscience

> We cannot reduce Jesus to natural sense perception. Matthew 28:18-20

The old creation - Adam is not a law unto itself. All power belongs to God. Isaiah 44:6, Isaiah 42:5-9

Verse 7 is showing us that the material sense of existence is a prison that keeps man bounded in discomfort.

> God – the object of our trust

> Christ – the power of our trust, the ability to maintain trust in God.

II Corinthians 12:9 – Grace is sufficient

Focus on grace, instead of the knowledge of good and evil. Psalms 139:12, Titus 1:15

I Thessalonians 5:23 Now we have faith, truth and life because of Jesus' nature within our spirit. We now focus on grace; which is God appearing first to the new spirit (Ezekiel 36:25), and then to the inward man (soul) and then to the body. If I am to be like Jesus, I must be in position to focus on grace. Isaiah 26:2

This life cannot abound without knowing Christ is life within. We cannot focus on the law of right and wrong. We must focus on what God has given us of his son Jesus within. Luke 17:20, I Timothy 1:7, Hebrews 2:14, Romans 5:1-5, I John 1:2-4, Acts 8 God has given us His life. Only he can maintain that life. Man's flesh cannot direct the life of God and Jesus. The soul must depend on the Holy Ghost to direct us. The only decision we make is to be willing to abide in his will, not the will of the flesh.

> ➢ There are two trees within us, but only one power. The power of God's love constrains me from walking after the knowledge of good and evil.

> ➢ Law of the sin in the body and a soul that is not renewed, Romans 12:1-3

We need the new man – Jesus – to feed the soul and realize the truth, which is in conscience.

Romans 8:10 The body is dead because of sin. The spirit is life because of God' righteousness.

I Corinthians 1:30 We must be willing to abide in his choice. John 15:1-7, John 15:16

Even we don't know everything he has given us. We must always be humble and meek; open to dwell in his presence. Be aware of his presence. Matthew 11:29-30 I must have the mind of Christ ruling within, depending on God only. Romans 6:6, Romans 8:16

➢ Separated from death – Genesis 2:17, Romans 8:1-3

We don't focus on good and evil because that nature was crucified with Christ on the cross.

Galatians 2:20-21 Now that the tree of knowledge has been dealt with by the cross, we now focus on the tree of life, not sin and death nature. We now focus on the righteousness of faith, now that the curse is removed - the cursed nature. Galatians 3:13, Philippians 3:9, II Corinthians 5:14-21

➢ Die daily to my will – all of this is flesh

- Human wisdom
- Human strength
- To the world

➢ The flesh

- Beast
- Self-centered

- Weakness
- Sin's dominion

➢ Deny the flesh, die to my fleshly understanding of right and wrong.

I ask you Father that your love constrain me. Check my spirit that I may abide in your and your word. Abide in me. Poses my soul. Luke 2:1-19, John 15:1-7

Expecting the Father to reveal himself in this vessel - Exodus 34:5-8

➢ Dead to the old nature

Romans 6:11, Matthew 22:37-40, Leviticus 19:18, Mark 12:31, Colossians 1:27

In Christ, love has fulfilled all the law and prophets. He fulfilled the negatives of the law; the "thou shalt <u>not do</u>" of the law. He also fulfilled the "dos" of the law, because he is of the nature that connects us to <u>grace</u>. The law - being condemnation of the <u>sin nature</u> - that is not subject to the commands of God's law, no condemnation. Romans 10:1-10, Romans 8:1-3 Thank God that the sin nature was put to death on the cross. Now in Christ, the sin nature does not have dominion over us. The Law of Moses - which dealt with the "do nots" - is no longer applied to us in Christ, the nature of righteous. Christ removed the cause of sin in our nature. In

Christ the negatives of the law don't exist, good and evil. Love removes the ability to do the negatives of the law. Christ's love covers the multitude of sin. Proverbs 10:12

All of the flesh's nature must be removed; the good as well as the evil of the tree of knowledge of good and evil. Both leads to sin. I Peter 4:1-3, Genesis 6:3

> ➢ Goal – Spiritual consciousness, but fist is identification Matthew 28:20, John 10:10, John 14:6, Hebrews 13:5, Luke 22:42

> ➢ Being released from material sense of consciousness, to consciousness of invisible spirit, omnipresence, all power, all knowing.

If I am to be an instrument for the invisible, I must be free from the world of material sense - the world of the five physical senses of fear and limitation. Knowing and being aware of the invisible spirit is the way to freedom. This must be first in all things. Man's spirit, soul and body must be recognized as the instrument by which the spirit is revealed - spirit of creation (God himself). Acts 17:22-31, II Timothy 1:7

Help me to be rid of the personal sense of self, apart from God's self. I am his temple. There is no separation of God from his creation – spirit. Material sense is a sense of separation from our source. That sense of separation causes us to be in the unrenowned mind; to be an actual separation, which is not the truth. Please help me to remember at all times, that you Father, your spirit is my individuality, expressing in soul and body. I must acknowledge the substance is invisible, appearing as whatever the need is, as food, supply, love, forgiveness, kindness, gentleness and goodness. Matthew 6:25-33, Romans 12:1-3

Observation of the five physical senses cannot be relied on as truth. Spirit within is life. John 6:63

> ➤ Walk by the spiritual impulse with in – right identification. I John 2:30

I must realize that my life lived according to mind and body cannot be relied upon as the life of identified in Christ Jesus. I must know my life is spirit of Christ within. I John 4:4 The world of our give physical senses keeps us bound up in a prison house of fear. That leads us into much discomfort. I must life by revelation of the Holy Ghost within my spirit, where trust is realized. The kingdom within must be realized. Luke 17:20-21 I must overcome the deception of belief in good. Humanhood must be denied. Only Christhood is sufficient. Turn away from the world of mind and matter to the realm of spiritual consciousness. Substance is the reality behind the form call faith. Hebrews 11:1-6 We do not go to God to solve human problems. Matthew 10:34-40, Luke 12:13-15 Only one reason to call upon God is God himself.

Tree of knowledge of good and evil is temporal judgement not spiritual. Devine grace appears as the need not give something. Grace forms itself as the need daily. Divine grace lives my life and I live as the beholder of the Glory of god on earth, which is fulfillment; to know I am one with the source, is Life.

Joshua 24:15, Matthew 6:24, John 18:36, John 17:15-16, Matthew 26:42, John 14:27, Matthew 19:17

Romans 8:7-8, Romans 7:15-17, I Corinthians 2:14, I Kings 19:18

Oneness must be recognized as the universe of truth – freedom form false perception of personal sense. Listen to the spirit. Infinity cannot be personalized. Divine spirit is the life of all creation. I must close the door of my five physical senses and commune with the spirit within. I Corinthians 2:9-16

Help me to practice this principal daily. Grace is freedom into something, not freedom from something. Freedom into the spirit of love, health supply, morals, mental, physical and financial. Colossians 1:27, Ephesians 4:24, Ephesians 2:1-10

Now we live for God to show his glory. Our need is always present. Philemon 6

I must choose not to accept belief in two powers. God in Christ is the only power. I must know that in the presence of God there is only one power. The other so called power exists only in a mind that is not renewed. Matthew 28:1-20 Awaken me Father! The kingdom of God is within. God is the only good among us. Colossians 3:12 Spirit is eternal – health, love, supply, obey, morals, forgiveness, gentleness and kindness is tree of life. Human health – temporal of the mind. Morals – knowledge of good and evil.

Carnal man forms the human identity - then takes anxious thoughts of how to maintain itself - whose life is based on the five physical sense for existence. This took place in the Garden of Eden, when Adam refused to be led by God's spirit. He lost his access to grace and truth, which is God revealed, giving form to the need. Matthew 6:25-33, II Corinthians 12:9 Taking thoughts for man's sense of existence does not produce the need. Man remains in a state of discomfort because of the lack of substance.

II Corinthians 1:12 – World testimony done away with Romans 3:31 – Faith, a channel from which the spirit flows

Desire to be righteous is of God.
Psalms 51
Deuteronomy 5:29
I Corinthians 1:30
Colossians 1:27
Psalms 115:1
11

# Proverbs 14:23, Proverbs 3:5, Matthew 28:19

So we see that mankind's prayers are based mostly on fear rather than the prayer of faith. We should be seeking God himself, instead of solving human problems. We must seek him, for him to be a witness to his glory. John 9:1-3 This act of healing was not for the blind man's person. Jesu mind was on God and the Glory of God was revealed. Matthew 6:25-33

I need the mind of Christ. Philippians 2:1-9, Hebrews 11:6

I need my mind stated on God to be more aware of the presence of the invisible more than the visible; no matter what form it is in. Please help me renew my mind. I Peter 1:22-23 Dominate my mind with the incorruptible seed within me.

- Isaiah 26:3, I John 2:20, Romans 8:14
  I John 2:2, I John 4:4, John 16:13-16

I must know God in spirit, in order for this to be done. I must have the spirit of Christ. Romans 8:9

II Corinthians 13:1-5. I must examine myself daily. Luke 9:23, Luke 11:13

God said he would give the Holy Spirit to them that ask of him, here God is saying the same thing in Matthew 6:25-33. The spirit is first because it is the spirit that gives life. What is his will appear by his grace. The spiritual person cannot expect that which is seen, touches by the hands or mind of man to be our life. God is spirit.

> ➢ Put off the human identity for the life principal.

> ➢ Transformation from human sense to spirit identification in Christ Romans 12:1-3, Ephesians 4:24

> ➢ Every born again child of God must seek to know his truth, identification in Christ.

In the beginning God created man in his image and likeness. Genesis 1:26-27 Adam was the man. Genesis 1:31 Adam was in line with God, spirit, soul and body. He was identified with God, who's existence was based on spiritual substance. Based on his obedience to God, depending on God's grace and truth. When Adam sinned, he willfully separated himself from God's grace or covering. After that came Adam's identification, which is earthly and made up of pairs of opposites,

- • Example of these:
  - o Sickness – health
  - o Poverty – wealth
  - o Companionship – loneliness
  - o Love – hate
  - o Likes – dislikes
  - o Life – death

Adam's material sense of existence is grounded in fear, based on the belief of a personal sense of "I", which in the kingdom of God is false perception of God's one world. Romans 12:1-3 The world of the natural man is based on man's ignorance of truth. In Christ we shall know the truth. Matthew 11:28-36 Adam separated himself from walking in the spirit of truth. Because of this, truth is not available to Adam; because he rejected God's grace. When he lost access to grace, he lost access to Life's principal. Without faith access, grace is denied. Hebrews 11:6 Adam forms the human identification. Since then man has anxious thoughts to maintain itself. If we are not more of the invisible than the visible, we will remain in a state of worry and fear. Genesis 3:10 We will remain in the state of the mind of self-preservation and self-covering.

We must rely on the wisdom of Christ; wisdom within the spirit. Walk in the grace of God revealed. To be free in grace, new creation people must realize the spirit, soul and body is of the same substance of God. The spirit is not sense observations. Luke 17:20-21

Father help me to put off the beliefs of the human identification, which is the first Adam. False perception of life in the spirit of God. Invisible spirit is my substance, character, nature – behold Jesus.

Hebrews 12:1-3, I Corinthians 1:30

Separate me from beliefs of the world of the five senses – physical. Ephesians 4:22-24, I John 2:16-17

Thank you for the Holy Ghost. Luke 11:9-13 Build my house. I Peter 1:10-12, I Peter 1:22-25, I Peter 2:4-6

The personal sense of "I" must be taken away. The personal sense of "I" causes discord. The creative principal of life did not create anything destructive to itself. Divine grace forms it's self as my daily need.

By this I am an instrument for God's activity of grace. Father help me to silence the earthly human thoughts within. Habakkuk 2:20, I Corinthians 6:19-20

> ➤ Put off the human.

Earthly man is shaped by the tree of knowledge of God and evil pairs of opposites. Tree of life is one.

Resist the golden calf in our mind. Have no reliance on anything except Christ, regardless of <u>appearance</u> to the five senses.

> ➤ Flee Babylon

Genesis 11:4 – Shows man's self-service.

Babel – confusion, the wisdom of man leads us away from Christ. James 3:15-16

The nature of carnal man cannot lead us to God. Jesus alone can lead us to God. Acts 4:12

This spirit of <u>Babylon</u> is in each person. Religion originated in the mind of man. That's why the religions systems is so large – hell enlarges, Isaiah 5:14. Flesh coves its own. The kingdom of God is rejected by man, John 18:36. We are to recognize no man or church according to the flesh, II Corinthians 5:16. Truth must be in us of Jesus, which is our freedom. In Christ, the leadership is not moved or intimidated by <u>challenges</u>. When over reacting to challenges, it is evident that one is not rooted in <u>Christ</u>. Unity is not based on <u>doctrines</u> that can be superficial. At best, only unity is in Christ Jesus. The Lord must be the focal point. We must focus on Christ. Examine all things – I Thessalonians 5:21. Look for what is right in Christ. We cannot be rude or abrasive with one who's in error, II Timothy 2:15, Psalms 119:160. I must seek to know the whole of God's word. Walking in truth is not just understanding, but abide in Christ who is truth.

Babel is the illustration of the pride of Cain's seed, believing in self-effort. Let us be like God. Man bows to many idols, but he has one god. Man himself – independent. Isaiah 14:13-14

Man must ceased trying to attain self-perfection. God wants us to look to him, have his nature by way of Christ Jesus, Philippians 2:6. At Babel, man's language was confused. At the Day of Pentecost they understood the language that testified of health. First <u>renew</u> the mind. It's the spirit that quickens! John 6:63, I Corinthians 2:1-16, II Corinthians 10:1-7

Matthew 22:37-40 When Jesus separated from the tree of the knowledge of good and evil, he fulfilled all the law and prophets. Now his love is my life. Christ is my life. Titus 1:15, Psalms 139:11-12

The old lineages of <u>Adam</u> has passed away by the cross of Jesus Christ.

<u>Divine grace</u> does not give us anything or manufacture anything for us. Diving grace appears as not sending something or giving something. Divine grace forms itself as my daily need. Divine grace appears as my spirit, soul and body. My flesh is nothing. Romans 5:1-5

I am one with my source, grace. God appearing, making up my whole being, wisdom, knowledge and understanding.

Man cannot <u>personalize</u> infinity or eternality. I can only bear witness to infinity. Thank God, life flows. I must be still to material sense and witness the spirit. Close the door to the five physical senses. Seek the <u>invisible</u> within, apart from the senses. Father help! Grace is the manna that always appears as the form necessary for the moment, spiritual, mental, moral, physical and finance freedom in grace. My prayer is to acknowledge God's grace that is always present. God with us, revealing himself. Help me to be a good and faithful witness.

Human make up, things, beliefs, theories, inhibitions, ignorance, prenatal, influences, superstitions of parents and grandparents from the time of birth. Make the choice – Grace remain in the world by abstaining from entering into its temptation. Help me to choose. I am an instrument by which God appears. Father awaken me to your omnipresence. Do not claim evil or good for self; but realize Christ within and grace abounds. Do not be carnal minded. I am not to claim any good or evil as self; but recognize grace the only power of Christ within. John 1:14-17 God is good all the time. We must acknowledge God's self and be his instrument of his <u>grace</u>. He appears as our everyday need. <u>Illusory</u>, world term is a false perception of the one <u>world</u> of God's creation.

Order of God in the new man come by revelation.

1. Spirit – reveals what is to be impulse apart from sense observation
2. Mental form - of what is to be
3. Material form – completes all, stars in the spirit 8:17, 18, 21 He referred to man's law of Moses. That was directed to the five physical senses, or flesh. The old family lineage lived life according to the outward life, where the soul is the principal of life; man's spirit was dead, unable to know or connect with the spirit of God.

Ephesians 2:1-6, John 6:63 Mankind must know the spirit of his existence instead of the fleshly observation of things for existence. Luke 17:20-21, John 4:24, Romans 8:14, John 7:16-19, Matthew 6:25-33, John 8:29-32 We are free in grace. John

1:17 The new family lineage does not seek its own, which is the world of the give physical senses. Luke 6:43

> ➢ Within me daily I Corinthians 11:28-32

In approaching my Father, I must put off the human identification, limited to the body and mind outward appearance. God does not patch up flesh. The carnal nature is not made better, but it must die.

The carnal perceptions of right and wrong – the tree of knowledge of good and evil

Our new identification is now the tree of life. Our focus is on Christ – our life. Colossians 3:4

Now that the curse is removed in Christ, we are fulfilled, in Christ, the law of - the do's and don'ts of the Law of Moses, which could not make us acceptable to God. Now we are accepted in Christ. Now having the spirit of Christ the very seed of life. I Peter 1:23 We have access to Grace. Romans 5:1-2 Remember that Grace is the spirit of God formed to glorify God at any time or place, situation and circumstances. Get used to practicing the presence of being in God's presence, trusting Him. He covers heaven and earth. There is no need to look outside of Him. He is the only power.

- Isaiah 57:15, I Kings 8:27

What causes mankind so much discomfort – man imputes power unto himself that is not power; such as sickens, poverty, being lonely, aging, etc. Not knowing where these thoughts come from. These imaginations come from the Garden of Eden when Adam broke from fellowship with God. Adam then believed in two powers. There is only on power! The other power is a false perceptions of the one power, as a man thinks in his heart so is he.

- Romans 14:14, Romans 12:1-3, Titus 1:15, Psalm 139:6-12

➢ The way to peace, is spiritual healing.

Exodus 34:1-11 I must know God is love. Goodness flows out from him all of the time. He is not a God that holds back his goodness from (family) his creation. Genesis 1:31 That good is his goodness revealed within his creation. Matthew 19:16-17 Man's approach to God must change. We must turn from approaching God with our body and mind as the object of our approach to God; meaning, for our sense of life.

➢ Example: healthy body, supply, food, clothes, finances, companionship.

- Matthew 6:25-33
- Luke 11:13

The body and mind approach cannot be the object of my approach to God. Romans 12:1-3

I must sacrifice my sense of existence. That has to be denied, Luke 9:23 I must know that I am dead and my life is hid in Christ. Colossians 3:1-6, Colossians 1:27, Galatians 2:20-21

In Christ, with God, my expectation is God and I realize that his grace is sufficient. II Corinthians 12:9

I must keep in mind that God my Father loves to impart himself to mankind. Jeremiah 9:23-24

He loves to show forth his goodness to and in his creation. The problem we are having today in not experiencing the presence of God started in the Garden of Eden. Man sought to cover himself with the knowledge of good and evil. There is no such thing in the righteousness of Christ. We must be willing to break away from the first family lineage to the last Adam, tree of Life. I Corinthians 15:34, 45-50

Spirit must bear witness. John 4:24, Ephesians 2:1-2 I cannot approach the spirit of God with a fleshly mind controlling me. My spirit must be in control, not the mind, and body. Ephesians 4:22-24

The mind and body does not dictate my approach to God, my spirit determines; that is how we sta in God's will. I John 3:19-24 God's desire is that he be revealed in us as instruments of his expression in mankind. John 8:28-32 I must be more aware of the presence of the invisible than the visible. It is the indivisible that is the life. Romans 8:18-25, John 6:63 I must maintain the thoughts. In Christ Jesus we are of a new family lineage. Luke 6:43 (Identity) Man's world is shared by the world of the five physical senses. Jesus made mention of this world of the five physical senses when he would say words in the scriptures. John

Psalms 139:12, Titus 1:15, Ephesians 4:4-6, Matthew 28:18-20 There's no opposite of infinity. Infinity is nothing else. Jesus' only desires were to glorify his Father in Heaven. No other desire than to please his Father all of the time. He focused on his Father's will. Purposed to walk by the invisible substance, provided by his trust in his Farther. That resulted in grace abounding. God has provided us with Jesus, the tree of life. I Peter 1:22, I Peter 3:4

If I am to live by the Father of the Son of God, I must have my whole desire and purpose to live for God's glory and nothing else. It has to be! These scriptures must be fulfilled in me. I must know my identity in Christ and conceive his attributes within my spirit. I must continue to be acquainted with god. Job 22:21 Job 23:14 God performs that which is appointed for me to do his commands.

Ecclesiastes 12:13, Colossians 1:27

# PART III

### Praise The Lord my Fellow believers
### In Christ Jesus our Lord, and Master.

I am writing my Thoughts, That The Holy Ghost has given me over Time. The Thoughts That I have Received are at Times difficult To articulate In Speech, so I have decided to write Them, To better point To The Truth, That The Lord has given Me In The Holy Ghost. The desire That The Lord has given me Is To Know The Truth of What happened In the garden of Eden with Adam and Eve concerning Man's Fellowship With God. In The Book of <u>Genesis</u> God said Let us Make Man. In our Image, and likeness, Image Is The character, Likeness Is the Substance, Gen. 1:26. Then In Gen 2:6 God Formed Man of The dust of the ground, and breathed Into his Nostrils The breath of Life, and Man became a living Soul. Man was In The Image of God, and Jesus, Man was perfect before God Gen. 1:31 Very Good It Was God because God's spirit gave Form To all That he created all creation bears God's character for what he wanted his creation to be, all creation bears his signature. The Moon, Stars, Water Ways, Mountains Just to Name a few, to This Day They Are all operating as he desires It to be, The only Creation of God that Is out of God's Will Is Man Kind. Man was given freewill, To Choose What God desired or what Man himself Desired God Set Life, and death before

Man (Adam). God Created Two Trees, or Two Family. Trees one Tree of Knowledge of good, and evil, one Tree of Life, We must recognize The <u>Sovereignty</u> of God in Which Is <u>Absolute</u> There Is No other Power, Is. 45:5-7

Prov. 16:4 The Lord Made all Thing for his Glory, all creation Is a Instrument Made by God To Show his glory, but all Must be In his order Then The Creation becomes a Partaken of God's glory If Man Is obedient To him. I have For Many years heard People Try To explain What happened In The garden of Eden To Cause God To Curse Adam, and Eve, some Say It was an apple, Some Say It was sex out of Season None of Man's reasoning can explain what happened, some say It was an angel from heaven, as I asked Questions, The More Their answers Confused People Than Could give The True explanation What happened In The garden of Eden. I began To Look at The Sovereignty of God, and realized When God Created These Family Trees, he Set In Motion The Consequences of each Tree The Trees of The Knowledge of Good, and evil, and The Tree of Life, When he created Adam, and Eve he set These Two Trees before Them, which represent Two Families, one righteous, and one unrighteous, Gen. 2:16-17. Now going To Gen 1:26 Adam was created First Formed From The dust of The ground which is the Body, next the Breathe of Life =The Spirit Which was not defiled. Then Following The breathe of Life Which was Adam's undefiled spirit, His spirit gave him a living soul, his soul was to receive direction From his undefiled Spirit That connected him To

God for Fellowship With God, Adam at That Time Knew only God's righteousness, having access To The Tree of life only. Adam Lived a Life of a Righteous Man obeying God's righteousness and being a Instrument of God's Glory revealed, as God showed Forth his attributes In Adam Exod. 34:5-8 This Is God's Plan for Man To Show Forth God's Image and Likeness In Mankind <u>I Cor. 13.</u> God's off springs Showing Their Father's glory one to another. That Is The Tree of Life, That is God's Will. The Tree of Life Fruit. Manifested by The Spirit of God's <u>Love</u>. Love Is Chief because <u>God is Love</u> out of The Spirit of Love comes all other Characteristics Matt. 22:37-40. Lev. 19:18 We cannot be caught up With So Much Knowledge That We pass over The Simplicity of God's word 2 Cor. 1:12, 2 Cor 11:3 Holy Ghost Tells us In 1 Cor 13:1-3, How easy It Is for man Kind To be caught up with Much Knowledge and Pass over The Most simple Thing required by The Lord.

As Long as Adam Conceived The Thoughts of God's approval for him to Please God bearing Witness To The Fruit or Character That Pleased God There was unbroken fellowship between God, and Adam.

Prov. 21:2

Prov. 20:27

Mankind must be careful That he comes To God To be a Instrument For God's Glory only The First Adam's focus was on self awareness good & Evil, seeking To Please self before

Man Kind, when we are born again We must Change our focus. From Self To God In Christ only <u>Luke 9:23</u>, Knowledge Alone puffs Man up, and He deceives himself, The result Is With That mind set Man's Knowledge Is In complete, so What Is needed Is Wisdom, The Spirit of Wisdom Which comes from God James 1:5-8 James 3:17-18 1 Cor. 1:30

The Lord Jesus, our wisdom Now He Has The Spirit without measure You See That The Spirit of Wisdom completes Knowledge, In order for our Knowledge To Manifeast The glory of God, Wisdom Must Confirm Knowledge In order To be effective In God's Life Changing Principal of God. In Man Kind, That's why Jesus Is our Wisdom Because he has The spirit Without Measure I Cor. 1:30, Matt. 28:17-20, we have our Measure To partake of his fullness John 1:16-17. The Spirit of Christ With In us gives us access to God's grace, which Is God himself. Rom. 5:1-5, Gal. 4:6, John 6:44-45 Jesus Spirit With In Us Is Sufficient to Keep us before. God Now We are No Longer Separated from Connection with God, Now that We have Died, The First Adam In Us Died on The Cross, With Christ Jesus, Rom. 6:5-10, We are Now Connected back To God In Christ, we have been connected back To God In Christ Jesus.

But When Adam Drifted away From God's Purpose, death entered In, and Separated Adam From God, This act Was a Willful disobedient act by Adam When he Conceived, The Thoughts Into his heart of The Tree of The Knowledge of good and evil This was Adam's Choice, God did warn him <u>Gen. 2:16-17</u> of The Consequences of <u>Disobedience</u> We Must Keep In Mind That God Created These Two Family Trees Long before Adam came Forth ??? God brought him forth WE recognize that, That one Tree Is <u>Single</u> = Tree of <u>Life</u>, and one Tree has (2) Two acts (1.) good (2) evil Pairs of opposites, Now some say That God Created These Two Trees one Negative, one positive, but That cannot be God Set before Adam Life, and Death. Adam's choice was Death by Conceiving The Thoughts of The Tree of The Knowledge of Good and evil, Adam brought Forth Death To all Man Kind after him Rom 5:12-16. God gave Adam The Power or ability To choose, and he Choose Death Instead of Life. Now getting back To The Point of Negative, and Positive We Know that cannot be If Positive, and Negative Thinking was God's Will, Why not allow The Tree of Knowledge of Good, and Evil to continue, as the way of Righteousness. It cannot be With God There Is No Positives, and Negatives. God Is one Way all The Time which Is Righteousness. God The Spirit of God Is <u>Infinity</u> <u>Infinity</u> has no opposites Infinity Is one Way only. The Thoughts That Adam Conceived In his heart Was The Law, as he Thought on The Law Prov. 23:7

everything that man calls good of Himself Is Absent of Christ's Highest Standard of Pure Morals, every Thing of Adam Is Vanity before God, We Need Jesus The New Man The Only Way To Please God Is by The Spirit of Christ With In Us. COL. 3:1-8, I must examine my heart daily to know That My dependance Is on God not Material Self, I Must Focus on The Spirit of Christ With In To Know I am In God's Presence and Not Man's Illusional Thoughts I Cor 13:5, Lk. 9:23

I must repeat What Adam bought Forth In The garden of Eden was The Law of Sin, and death The Tree of The Knowledge of Good, and Evil

* Law of Sin and Death (Power) of Sin Source is God's Law I Cor 15:57

* Law of Moses Knowledge of man's heart before God Rom. 3:20-31 Knowledge of Right and wrong

The word <u>Devil</u> Is a word That has Many Meanings, and Many have Misunderstood What The Devil Is or What Is expressed by The use of The Word Devil, going back to The garden of Eden, What Adam Did was To Oppose The Commandment That God gave him Concerning <u>Life</u> and <u>death</u>, I will repeat What I have written all ready Number one The Commandment was given Gen. 2:17 Adam was Told What Would happen He disobeyed God, he was given access To The Tree of Life, Which was God's Will for Adam, and his off springs after Him, The Tree of Knowledge of Good, and evil was also Set before him, he was given Free will, To chose for himself Life or Death, Adam was to choose, But his choice was not only for himself, but all Man Kind after him Would be What Adam chose between These Two Trees his choice would be The Life of all humanity after Adam was The seed by what he Chose, Adam was To be The Life of all born after Him He's The spiritual Father of all The Children born of a Woman In to The World from The day he disobeyed God Unto the Present Time

* John 8:44 Jesus Called Adam Their Father The Devil, Adam Was Called The Devil because he Opposed God's Commandment, and Placed The Focus on himself, When Jesus told Them That They were of Their Father The Devil, Which Is The Nature of Adam, This Is Man Kind Spiritual Condition when They are born Into The World now That word <u>Devil</u>, <u>Satan</u>, <u>Lucife</u> Means The some which Is to oppose The Righteousness of God's Commandments, So we see Adam brought Sin Into The World Rom. 5:12-16 We Must Remember The Cause and, effect of Man's Condition In The World Today, Now We Know That Man Born after he became What The law Was against <u>Prov. 23:7</u> he By Knowledge of Good and Evil be came a Transgressor, by disobeying God's Command not To eat or Conceive The Law IN his heart, by Disobeying God he became an out Law, Thus becoming a servant of sin <u>I Tim. 1:9-10</u> Now What Adam Conceived In his heart Is Revealed In The law of Moses. Book of <u>Exodus</u>, <u>Lev Deut</u> This Is What Caused Adam To be The Servant of Sin.

I Say That he Is a servant of Sin because of Sin's Power I Cor 15:57 Source That Power Source Is God's Law, Adam The Carnal Man or fleshly Man, Is a servant of Sin who's Strength

Is God's Law against Unrighteousness of Adam. The Fleshly Man or Carnal Adam has No Power Rom: 7:23

Sustain himself, before God and Man, Act 24:16 The Law In Rom 7:23 Is The Power, That The Children of The First Adam must be Released From, We cannot Gal 3:13 and will not Do away With The Law We Must Die, The Carnal Man or Nature Must Die So That The righteousness of The Law Can be Fulfilled In Us <u>Matt. 5:17</u> by The Spirit of Christ The New Nature Eph. 4:22-24 If We are To be perfect as our Father Is Mt. 5:48 Perfect We Have To get To The Place Within us That There Is No Knowledge of Good and Evil but one Spirit With The <u>Lord</u> Looking at The Scriptures Ps. 139:12, Titus 1:15. We Must be empty of all self awareness, and be completely walking daily In The awareness of God Only because Adam's Knowledge only Caused him To Focus on self awareness In stead of worshipping God Only John 4:23, Out of Self awareness comes LUST of Flesh, LUST of Eyes, Pride of Life Not of The Father <u>I John 2:15-17</u> When Adam Lost The fellowship he had with God he made The attempt to Cover himself with Material Things Instead of depending on God's glory To Cover him Gen 3:1-24, That Same Spirit Is With us Today every child born of a woman has This very same spirit of Carnal Adam. We Must be born again of Water, and Spirit Jn. 3:1-8 Acts 4:12. Man's Weak Fleshly Nature Is Nothing, It does Not Matter Who We are or What we can do all In The eyes of God is Vanity Ps 39:5

Man and Impart his Grace, Grace comes In our Life, by Faith of The Spirit of Christ with In, We must respect God's way Spirit To Spirit No Flesh To Spirit our God Is one way his way I Cor 2:19-14 James 1:5-7 We see That Faith brings forth God's grace That God has for Jesus. As Children of God we are clothed from with In us First Spirit, Then Soul, Then The body purification begins with In The Spirit of Man. We must know God as our Father, Not our creater only, God is The creater of all, but he's Not The Father of all, he's The father of all That have The Spirit of his only begotten Son Jesus, Gal. 4:6 we cannot Stress This Point enough. We need The Spirit of Christ and We must know That We must know by revelation That we Have The Spirit of Christ

Exodus, Leviticus, Numbers, Deuteronomy The law did not lead man to perfection but Showed Man exactly Who he Is gave him, Knowledge of his Sin Nature Rom. 3:19, Rom. 3:10 Rom. 3:20 There is only one To blame For The Pain, and suffering of all Man Kind, That Is Adam, Nothing else, The Law was our school Master to bring us to Christ Gal. 3:24 In Christ We are Accepted by God Eph. 1:3-7, We see that There are Two Laws one of Sin and death Rom. 8:2, Law of Moses Is The Second Law Which shows Man What a wretched Man he Is. The Law Made No Man Perfect, but bring In a New Life Heb 7:19

* Now The Third one Is The Law of The Spirit of Life In

Christ Jesus Rom. 8:2, Rom. 6:3-7 Now In Christ Jesus we have Freedom In God's

The cursed Nature of Adam can not do God's Righteousness even If he desires to do good, because of his cursed Nature he's Not a vessle of righteousness of God, because the righteousness of God Must be In The Heart Those of The Nature of Adam are cursed Gal. 3:13 even If he wants To Do God's Righteousness he cannot The lawless Spirit of Adam cannot do The Righteousness of The law of God's Righteousness Is. 64:6, Ps 39:5 Man's Sinful Nature Cannot Please God Rom. 14:23 Rom 7:18-19 We See In Scriptures Show us That Without Christ In Us We can Do Nothing Jn. 15:5. Because of The Sin Nature of Adam We are Nothing before God, Cannot Serve Him God Did Not bring Sin Into The World, but his Creation of The Tree of The Knowledge of Good and Evil brought Forth The Power of Lawlessness By Adam Sin entered

The law of Sin and Death came by Adam, God did not Impute Sin even Through he Rom 4:8 created The Tree From Which Sin Came From Gen. 3:1, So you can not serve God, By Just Knowledge of man's understanding of Right and Wrong. Man must have The Spirit or Nature of God's Righteousness with In his heart or Spirit. Man Kind after The Fall of Adam, Man's Spirit was Dead To The Leading of God's Spirit With In, Adam Became a man of The Flesh called Fleshly or Carnal which means Adam's Life Dependance was on The soul's observation of The Five Physical senses Lust of The Flesh, Lust of The eyes, Pride of Life, The Soul of Man cannot be The Principal of Man's Life, because The Soul Is a Instrument for The revelation of God's Spirit In First God Reveals his Thoughts To Man, Then with The Mind Man is given understanding, Then execution Through The Body of Man Kind.

We have To be Willing To Let go our will of The Flesh, and approach God for God Then he will Reward us with him self, he will give form to The Need by his Spirit, All Things were made for Him Col. 3:16-18, Remember Matt. 6:25-33 Seek The Kingdom of God First Rom. 14:16-17 Seek God, The Manifestation of The Spirit of The Kingdom with In The New Spirit Ez 36:25-27, Luke 17:20-21 I just see God he Did not create This world, and Every thing with In it Heb. 11:3 by Things That Was In existence, he spoke It Out of his heart or spirit. God is Willing, and Loves To help us but It has To be The way he Is Jere. 9:23-24, Nothing else Lam. 3:22-27, To Remove all fear We must Seek To Renew Our Minds so The Spirit of God Is In Contact With Man Kind

God does not Impute Sin, God gave Adam The ability To Choose The destiny of Man Kind, he gave Adam a choice of one Family Sin and Death, and Tree of Life When God Created These Two Trees, he gave Man a free will, and What ever Adam chose God's spirit was The source of What was chosen Is. 45:5-7 Remember That God Made all Things For himself Prov. 16:4, God Made all things, and The Consequences for

The Choices we Make, We Set In Motion The Consequences of our Choice, God Tells Us What To choose Deut. 30:19-20. God gets No Glory out of Man Kind dieing Ez. 18:23, 32 Death according To God Is To be separated from Him. When Adam disobeyed God he Died, and all after Him were Separated as he is In Adam all Die I Cor. 15:22

Because Adam's Undefiled Spirit was In Contact With God, but When Adam broke fellowship With God In his Spirit he had To depend on The observation of Five Physical senses For his covering Gen. 3:7 This Is The Result of The Law In his heart Instead of The Spirit of God's Commands Adam discovered In The Law That It was Not Lawful To be unclothed so he Tried To obey his Sense of righteousness instead of God's righteousness Adam's Nature was Lawless because he chose The Law over Righteousness The Law Is Not for The Righteous I Tim 1:8-10, This Is The Nature Adam chose To Live by The law, but by Adam's disobedience The Law became a curse, he could Not Control The Lawlessness In his heart, because He did Not have Faith of God Rom 3:20, Heb. 11:6

With God's Spirit, Because We Have The Spirit of Christ Within us. Rom. 12:1-3 We must Renew our Minds, Now That we have The Spirit of Christ Instead of Adam II Tim. 1:7, I John 4:17-18 Heb. 2:14-18, as my Spirit Is connected To God's Spirit My expectation Is God, His Will In This body God's Temple I Cor. 6:19-20 That being The case There's only <u>One Will</u> Not The Will of The Flesh, but <u>God's Spirit</u>. I must put off My thoughts, opinions, Fears, and be a coLaborer of God, In Christ, even If I have These Thing comforting Me That Is Common To Man I must Keep My Focus on God The Spirit Instead of Fleshly Mind of Man The Main Problem Is Man's Un Renewed mind after Conversion We Must Change our approach To God. God Is Too Holy To Look On Man's unrenewed Mind of Flesh God has given us a New Spirit so That we can Stay In Contact with Him Ez. 36:25-27

grace by Jesus Christ by Faith Rom. 5:1-3 Heb 7:11-12 Heb. 8:16-13, These scriptures That I write are To edify God's People, and Show The grace, and Mercy of God To Man Kind Upon The earth Eph. 2:1-13. Jesus Is our Salvation, Meaning he Is everything I need To Please God our Father In Christ We Must Keep In Mind That God has accepted Us In The Spirit of Christ, We Need To Maintain Fellowship with God our Father, We Must Know God Is our Father once we receive The New Birth, John 3:1-8, Then Go on To receive The Baptism of The Holy Spirit, Power To bear, or is of witness to the spirit of Christ within acts 1:8, Acts 2:4 Acts 8:14-17, Now That The Spirit has been poured out every soul, that has the New birth can Receive The Holy Ghost first Man must acknowledge Jesus Death, burial and Resurrection Is What They believe as Their Justification To dwell In God's Presence will he saved Rom 10:9-10, Mark 16:16-18, Now When Man Kind receives The word of God, and believes That Jesus Died for Their Sins They Shall be Saved or Justified In Christ, Then go on to be baptized In The Holy Ghost.

1. Repentance
2. Water baptized
3. Receive The Holy Ghost baptism you must go to God, and Receive The Spirit The Spirit has already been given, Just acknowledge, God's is willing To give us his Spirit Luke 11:13 We are his Sons If we Look To Jesus To be our Salvation John 6:39-40, Gal. 4:6

If I am To please God I must have The Spirit of Christ Jesus To be My Life This Life Is To Be a Witness of God's attributes of our Father Exodus 34:5-8, These attribute of God are revealed In Christ Jesus Not Only To Jesus but all That have received The Spirit of Christ I Cor. Chapter 13, Reveals what we have Inherited from God In Christ, John 8:28-29 We must be willing To Sacrifice time, and Pleasure To Continue In God's Word, and Spirit Jesus Is The Word of God his Spirit With In Us Is Spirit, and Life John 6:63, This Scripture Is Not for Jesus alone by all That have The Spirit of Christ With In 2 Cor. 13:4-5 We must know this making our Calling Sure. Truly God's grace Is sufficient, To supply every one of his Children With What ever The Need Is

Example Water To Wine Book of John Chapter Two Feeding The Five Thousand Matt. 14:14-21

Healings That Took Place In Jesus Ministry, also The apostles shows us that When there is a Need In The Lives of His Children he Will be The Need Seek Him Heb. 11:6 Seek God The (Spirit) Not What Man Perceives To be The Need by way of Sense observation The Spirit forms it Self as The Need Seek The Spirit of God be a Faithful and True Witness. Expect The Unseen The Spirit of Creation Rom. 8:24-25, 2 Cor. 4:18, Focus in God The Spirit, The Way To focus on The unseen With The Spirit The New Man Eph. 4:24 Is to Ask God To Remove from My Mind all fear, ask him to reveal his Strength In my weakness, There Is a Lot of Praying, and Very little Results other Than More Pain, and Suffering

Adam's Spirit being Dead to God's Spirit No longer can Receive God's direction, so he now has To depend on his soul's observation Intellect, Will, emotion The law of Sin In his Members Is now The life which he lives Rom 7:23 Law of Sin In his Members, made up of The Five Physical senses The Soul of Man Now depends on his soul's observation at self preservation, When The Soul Is used for The life Principle The End Is Not Peace Is. 57:20-21 God's peace In Man Is Eternal Life, man's Peace Is Temporal. If The Soul of Man Is The Life Principle here Is What happens

1. Fleshly Man (sinFul)
2. Soul The Life Principal
3. Nature expressed Is Sinful We Just discussed The Law of Sin and death knowing That Their's Nothing external To man Is What causes Man To be Separated from God Matt 15:10-11, Mark 7:14-23

So Put To rest The Theory That There Is a being out side of Man That Causes Man To be Separated From God, No It's

What Adam conceived In his heart That caused him To be a Lawless creature In The Presence of God Adam The Man John 8:44 and his Lawless Nature has been Passed on To every Child born In To The World Rom. 8:2

The Law of Moses Is Not God Imputing Sin To Man, What God revealed To Moses Is The Condition of Man's heart That Adam conceived and Passed Onto all Man Kind, So We See The Law of Sin, and death Came by Adam The Law of Moses shows What Is In The Heart, The Law of Condemnation. The Court of Man's Law Is an Indictment true bill The Law of Moses Shows Man's Nature In The Books of The Law Shows all Man Kind guilty before God

I must keep In mind that Man did not bring Forth what he's suffering Today on Themselves but This what is happening Today because We Inherited From Adam In the garden of Eden. Rom. 5:19 What was passed on to us was The law of Sin, and death.

Rom 8:2, This law of Sin and death came about because Adam wanted to be Judge Himself as he ate from The Tree of The Knowledge of Good, and evil, eating means To conceive Thoughts In The heart, Then expressed In The soul of Man Kind, Now Looking at The result of Adam's disobedience man was reduced To The law Ecc. 3:18-20 animal Like condition, murder stealing, lying destroying one another for selfish gain, which is self preservation, Instead of trusting God for existence In The garden before The fall God's glory covered Adam, and Eve

Note: The law of God is the life, the power, the ability of God revealed, no matter the form, the power of life is God, the power of death is God all power is of God whether it is life or death ISAIAH 45:6-7, 1 Corinthians 15:56 to man kind God's power is revealed according to the choice man kind makes Deuteronomy 30:19-20, all of the effects of man's choice is predestined no matter what the the choice is life or death God is the Source of all, Proverbs 16:4. We see in God's word that there is no separate entity no power out side of God's power no existance out side of God's power John 19:11 no other power for good or evil every thought we take, and conceive in our heart the effects of our conception is already predestined by God, and every decision the out come has already been determined by God Ezekiel 11:5, 1 Chronicles 28:9. God knows all because he put those thoughts there. People say the devil did this, and that the only devil is Adam's sin nature a lawless creature, an opposer of God's commandments there is no other creature other than Adam's cursed sin nature. Adam's sin nature is the curse of God's law to man kind, Jesus is the righteousness of the law because of his obedience to God's commandments, because of his obedience the law of God is fulfilled Matt. 22:37-40, Matt. 5:17, cast out the fables and walk in truth of God not man's fables, 2 Cor. 10:3-7, 3 John 1:3 search out what you hear by searching the scriptures to know what is truth Acts 17:11-13. Another example that Adam's temptation was not from something external to himself, is found in Luke 4:1-13 these temptations were thoughts in Jesus mind there was nothing out side of him tempting him, JESUS said in the book of Mark 7:14-23 where these temptations come from, the serpent nature housed in the human body that feeds the mind with its thoughts. The law of the sin nature is in the physical body of all humans ROMANS 7:23, GEN. 3:1-5 Adam was tempted when he was drawn away of his own lust and enticed JAMES 1:13-16. JESUS was tempted with the same temptations as Adam Heb. 4:15 but Jesus did not sin. Jesus in the pattern for all of man kind to please God. We must look to Jesus, and him only for our salvation ACTS 4:12. There are those that will dazzle you with all kinds of words, but no substance of God supplied by the Spirit of GOD ONLY. 1 Cor. 2:1-15, man will always project himself into the scriptures instead of the simplicity of the gospel of Jesus Christ 2 Cor. 11:3. Receive revelation knowledge with in your spirit given by the Holy Spirit then you will KNOW THE TRUTH, THAT IS YOUR FREEDOM. JOHN 8:31-32. TRUTH IS WITH IN BY REVELATION NOT BY HEAD KNOWLEDGE, LUKE 17:20-21. Put on the new man Eph. 4:22-24. Ask God to reveal himself with in the spirit of the new man, That is in the image of CHRIST JESUS. AMEN.

## With his stripes we are healed Is. 53:5

This scripture has been used out of context for hundreds of years, people have used this scripture to apply to the physical body, instead of the focus being on the spirit of God. God's desire for his born again children is that we focus on God the spirit to bring mankind back to the place he had with God, before Adams Transgression in the garden of Eden. Before Adam sinned his focus was on God the spirit, which caused his spirit, soul, body to be whole no sin and death no discomfort at all in Adam, and Eve. Gen. 1:31 states that all of God's creation was good, and very good totally in line with God's righteousness. No lack of anything just the pure life of God in Adam, God's righteousness was manifested, and it was all good. Adam's transgression brought sin into world of man. and separated man from being a witness of God's comfort, to mankind. After Adam's sin in the garden Adam was no longer in fellowship with God he lost his access to God's grace because of his disobedience, upon his disobedience his focus was directed to being covered with the tangibles such as fig leaves before his transgression he was covered from within with God's spirit Gen. 3:6-11 when he conceived the law in his heart which is the tree of the knowledge of good, and evil. The law is holy and good the problem with Adam is that his disobedience brought forth the curse of the law upon act mankind, new after his fall he became as a animal (beast nature) a beast cannot relate to God's spirit only mankind was created to relate to God's spirit. Adam became a beast, with the beast nature he can only relate to what his five physical senses reveal, with that nature he seeks to cover himself with the material sense of existence, just as the animals in the jungle praying on others weaknesses for survival the ability to live above the animal instincts for survival Ecc. 3:18-22. Adam's intent was to conceive the law of God in his heart, and he as God Gen 3:5, The problem with his thinking was that the knowledge of Good, and Evil would not put him in right standing with God, the substance was missing because of the curse he received, because of his transgression of the law, Is. 64:6 Adam's cursed nature can only produce the curse of the law, Is. 64:6 Adam's curse can only produce more unrighteousness. There's a desire within man to do right but because of man's cursed nature, man cannot produce God's righteousness.

Man cannot approach God with the mind of Adam, because Adam's focus is on the outward man, because he can only approach God according to his nature within, and that nature cannot fellowship with God. When mankind seeks God he fails because without faith it's impossible to please God, man must be born again, and approach God in the faith at the Lord Jesus Christ because God's promises are to Christ, and those that have the spirit of Christ Heb. 11:6 that is why I said instead of approaching God with the mind on self preservation of the five physical senses we must approach him with the mind of Christ one who walk by faith the spirit of faith within us God acts directly within our new spirit which is Christ Jesus Col. 1:27 then from within the spirit God's grace is manifested to the soul and body, when Isaiah 53:5 says that by his stripes we are healed he is saying that the cursed nature is removed so that we no longer walk according to the five physical senses but the inward witness of the spirit of Christ within which is our salvation we are healed with the spirit of Christ within us our spirit is live in Christ before the spirit of Christ came we were bound by the observation of the five physical senses Gae. 3:13, 23 and the observation of the five physical senses do not give us the exact knowing that is necessary, because the five physical senses are housed in the soul. The soul cannot be the place where truth is revealed, that is why we must be born again of the water, and spirit John 3:3-8 means that man's spirit must be made alive in Christ Jesus Eph. 2:1-10, Eph 4:22-24 if we follow the pattern of Christ in the scriptures John 7:37-39 once we realize Christ Jesus teaching on how to approach God's righteousness we will have the true comfort that God desires us to have, he wants to bless his children but we must follow his order. Healing comes first the spirit, soul, body I Thess. 5:23 by his way we can be witnesses as Christ Acts 1:8. If we live according to the five physical senses we die Rom. 8:13 having the spirit of Christ we live, we are believers, 2 Cor. 4:13 I Pet. 1:21 Remember that we know God within our spirit, we understand with the mind to be established in God's kingdom not meat, and drink only Rom 14:17, Matt. 6:33, body healing, mind healings will be manifested by the spirit of Christ within.

The law of sin and death came by Adam's disobedience, as the result Death came in to mankind Rom 5:17-19. The sin nature is the rule of all mankind as the result death is what mankind reaps the wages of the sin nature is death Deut. 30:19-20 God is not to be blamed for this death God does not impute sin, and unrighteousness to mankind Rom. 4:6-8.

The law of sin and death is not Gods will for mankind. God is the power source for all Is. 45:5-7

The Law of Moses revealed man to himself, exposed man's nature, showed why man could not dwell in God's presence, Rom. 3:19-20, the sin nature hinders us. Moses was given the law to show man what was in his sin nature, as we read the first five books of the Bible what we see is God telling mankind what not to do because of Adam's seed. Rom. 7:23 Heb. 7:19, 2 Cor. 3:6-7 The letter of the law is to one who walks according man's natural, intellect, will emotions without the spirit within which is Christ Jesus. The law of Moses is not God's will for mankind. God is the power source Is. 45:5-7, The law of Moses revealed to mankind the need for redemption in Christ Jesus 2 Cor. 5:18-21. Rom. 3:24.

The law of the spirit of life in Christ Jesus Rom. 8:1-4, Now that Jesus became as we yet without sinning he never yielded to sin nature John 8:29 Jesus had the sin nature so that he could pay the price of redemption for mankind. He knew no sin meaning he did not become intimate with the sin nature being tempted yes but he never sinned against God. Now some one may ask what does the scripture say that he became sin 2 Cor. 5:21 To reconcile us to himself God made Jesus to be sin so that God's righteousness could be within us. Jesus gave up his righteousness so that we would be born again into Jesus righteousness by faith for the purpose of being reconciled to God, Jesus was without sin he could not die, he laid down his life. John 19:11, the law of the spirit of life in Christ Jesus is God's will for mankind we see this is God's will from the beginning that man was created by God for life eternal Gen. 1:31 John 14:6 Adam was in Christ Jesus man is in the image of God the father, God in Christ has taken us back to that place that Adam had before he sinned. The image is available to all that confess Jesus to be their Lord and Savior.

Brothers and Sisters in Christ Jesus we are now accepted by God in the spirit of Christ Jesus Ephesians 1:1-7, the death of Jesus Christ has removed the curse of the law that Adam brought in mankind now through the death, burial, and resurrection of the Lord Jesus Christ we have access to God our Father in heaven by the spirit of Christ Jesus who is our life in Christ is the righteousness of the law giving us access to God Romans 5:1-2 The curse of God's law is removed, praise god for giving us access to the very spirit of peace John 14:27 we must remember that Jesus Christ is our life Psalm 84:11 the good thing is in Christ Jesus, we must acknowledge every good thing within us in Christ Jesus Philemon 6. Now we can draw near to God with a pure heart in Christ Hebrews 10:22 Isaiah 32:17.

In conclusion please seek to know the truth given by God's spirit in the new creation life in Christ. The lord has put it in my heart to know the truth that is in the spirit of the Lord Jesus Christ, we cannot allow what man's wisdom Teaches but what the Holy Ghost teaches I Cor. 2:6-7. The holy ghost reveals the truth that is in us by Christ Jesus I John 2:20, 27, John 16:13-14 let us depart from fables given by man's earthly wisdom, let us ask in faith of Jesus Christ to show us plainly of the Father John 16:25. Hebrews 8:10-13. We must read our bibles, pray, fast as we seek God with all our heart we will know him Jeremiah 29:11-14, get Job 22:21. We must work out our salvation in reverence of God in the image of Christ Jesus. I am grieved when I see my brothers, and sisters trying to please God with self effort, trying to put on a good human appearance instead of trusting in Christ Jesus faithfulness, we are not trying to be good humans, we are being transformed into the image of Christ Romans 12:1-3. The Human appearance walk by sight, but we that are in Christ walk by faith. We must be removed from the illusion of a material existence, God is not a material God, God is spirit John 4:24 God does not depend on the material Heb.11:3 but the spirit which gives form to the need at hand 2 Cor. 4:18 God did not create this world by what was already in existence Heb. 11:3 Rom. 8:24-25 God spoke this universe into existence himself. Now in Christ Jesus we are to have the same mind in our dependence on him we are not our own I Cor. 6:19-20, 2 Cor 6:15-18. In Christ we live Acts 17:28 Phil. 2:5-9. As born again citizens of heaven we are no longer under the illusion that this material world is our life, God is the spirit that has created us in Christ Jesus to know, and worship the creator instead of worshipping the material, and believing that it is Life, the spirit of God is the beginning and the ending. All glory belongs to the spirit visible and invisible for him, and by him the spirit. Let us press on and the thankful that we are his image. Continue to trust God. Now that, we are his children in Christ Jesus. God bless you all that read this book.

* The curse of the Law of God, and its effect on the whole human race. When God created Adam, and Eve. God wanted them to have eternal life. Free of Corruption. The perfect of life of God himself nothing else. When God instructed Adam concerning the Tree of Knowledge of Good, and Evil, and the Tree of Life, he told Adam what would be the consequences of his choice. The Tree of Life is Life eternal, and the Tree of the Knowledge of good and evil is death Gen. 2:16-17 God commanded Adam what Tree to chose from. The Tree of the Knowledge of Good, and Evil The law, Adam was created in the Image of God perfect, there was no law needed The Law did not apply to Adam the Law is not for a Righteous Man 2 Tim. 9-10, but when Adam sinned by disobeying God's Commandment he became a lawless creature before God he lost his perfection. Adam brought corruption into the world all mankind suffered the consequences of Adam's choice Rom. 5:12-13. Adam lost communion with God Gen. 3:8-11 he also lost the ability to receive Revelations from God, because he was spiritually dead, and could not receive Revelation Knowledge, and wisdom from God, all that Adam had left was the knowledge of right and wrong, even with the knowledge of right and wrong, even with the Knowledge of Right, and Wrong he could not please God because when he disobeyed God he was cursed, his Nature was of a Curse Nature and could not walk with God in Faith, and without Faith if is impossible to Please God Heb. 11:6 He became a non believer. He became a carnal man animal like creature fleshly, temporal dependence, instead

of spiritually dependant or God the spirit <u>Rom. 8:5-8</u>, <u>Ecc. 3:18-22</u>. Adam could no longer be led by God's Spirit with in him Prov. 20:27. So he could only depend on his Sense observation depending on material things as Life which is temporal not eternal life source in God. Because of Adam's Cursed Nature he was bound to live a Life of Corruption the sin Nature ruled him his soul was bound to the Curse of Law even though he had conscience of Right, and Wrong he could not do the righteousness of the law, only the Curse which is given in the Law of Moses <u>Exod. 20:12-17</u> The Law of Moses revealed man's Cursed Nature, and that Nature can only produce the lawlessness of Man's Nature <u>Rom. 5:20-21</u>, even if one desires to do the righteousness of God's Law he cannot because of the Lawless Nature can only produce after its kind <u>Rom. 7:12-25</u> The power that rules the Sin Nature is God's Law <u>I Cor. 15:56</u> the only way to freedom is death of the Sin Nature just trying to do the Law with the Sin Nature is non productive, the Sin Nature must die Rom. 8:3-4. Every tree produces after its kind. God's Law cannot be done away with, It's there to stay man must acknowledge Jesus, and believe the Jesus died for our Sin Nature, and the curse on mankind. <u>Gen 3:13-14</u> Mankind must acknowledge this fact in order to be saved. Jesus is the only way for Mankind to dwell in the presense of God's righteousness by faith, Jesus died to bring us to God our Father, <u>Gae. 4:1-6</u>. We must remember that whatever we choose whether Death or Life the effects of our choice is already in place predestinated every thought is from the Lord <u>I Chronicles 28:9 ISAIAH</u>

<u>45:5-7</u> We must be careful concerning our thoughts, because as God has established Moon, Stars, Oceans, and these actions, and habitation he has also established man, and man's habitation, and thoughts are also established by God himself, our thoughts have consequences when God created man he put everything in place he need not watch us. The watch has already been established when he created man, we are vessels some to honor, some to dishonor <u>Deut. 30:19-20</u> <u>Is. 46:10</u> <u>Ecc. 3:11</u> <u>Isaiah 41:4</u>, <u>Acts 17:26</u> Man Kind must realize, that nothing originates with man, we are the vessels created by God to chose Life or Death, and which one we choose the consequences are already in place even our next thought is for is to choose or not to choose that is why we are instructed to learn of Christ Jesus our example, and Lord. When we follow the pattern so that we are pleasing to God our Father, we want our thoughts to be of Christ Jesus to give us Rest for our Souls <u>Matt. 11:28, John 5:39.</u> In Christ the Curse is removed now we are accepted by God being in Christ <u>Eph. 1:6 7</u>. Man Kind must realize his place, and submit to God, and allow the Holy Spirit to instruct us according to God's will IJN. 2:20, 27 do not rely on man's intellect for direction but depend on the Holy Spirit to lead us in all Truth. With Christ being our life we have access to grace, now that the Curse of the Law is taken away by the Cross of Jesus our Lord, now the Righteousness of the Law is fulfilled in the Spirit of Christ. We come now boldly to the Throne of God's Grace. <u>Heb. 4:14-16</u>. <u>Rom. 5:1-5</u> <u>Gae. 3:23-29</u>

Know that we are Dead in Christ, the UD Adam Nature, in now dead in all who trust in Christ Jesus who delivered us from Death I Cor. 1:10, when Jesus took us to the Cross he destroyed the Sin Nature within Man Kind John 16:25, Col. 3:1-3, Heb. 2:14 Thank God that Jesus died for Man's Sin Nature, now that we have the Nature of Christ Jesus we can purify our souls I Pet. 1:18-25, Rom 6:11

Having a New Spirit
What does it mean
Eg. 36:25-27

First of all we must always remember that we are now horn again we must change our belief from observation of the five Physical Senses to the Inner Man of the Spirit, now that we have access to God given within us. We must be led by the Holy Spirit within our New Spirit which is Christ Jesus, called the New Man Ephesians 4:23 24, Rom. 8:14-17. Which is Christ Jesus within Col. 1:27. The Holy Spirit is here with in us to reveal God's will manifesting. The Kingdom, Luke, 17:20-21 Rom. 14:17-18, our Spirituals Faculties are given to know the ways of God for us within us. Apart from being led by The Holy Spirit within our New Spirit there is no other way to please God. God will only communicate with Man Kind, with in the New Spirit within us. In the Image of Christ John 14:6, Acts 4:12.

Now that we have our Spiritual Faculties give to us, we now have the ability to know God.

1. Intitution ability to be led by the Spirit of God I Cor. 2:9-16, Rom. 8:14 our Faculty of Intitution receives God's will then once God's will is received, our Conscience bears witness to what has been received from the Holy Spirit within our Spirit, that becomes the Word of God, Man Kind can read, study but will miss the Will of God, the word only becomes life when we receive communication within Intitution, and our Conscience bears witness to what the Holy Spirit has revealed with the New Man. Intitution is where the Will of God is revealed, the becomes our will, this must possess our Soul's will Luke 21:19, we see that the opposite of the Soul's Will is the Spirit's will of Intitution.

Opposite of the Soul's Will is Intitution's Will received from the Holy Spirit within we must know that the Soul is given understanding the Soul is not given the knowing directly from God. God does act directly upon Man's New Spirit which is exact knowing, then the Soul is given understanding Prov. 3:19, Prov. 4:5-7 Job. 28:28. We must seek the Kingdom of God Matt. 6:33

2. Conscience Function is to discern what has been revealed by the Intitution by the Holy Ghost. Conscience expresses the Holiness on in Word Monitor in the Spirit of Man Kind concerning divine Nature. Conscience is the Organ of Faith, where substance is located, for instance if one is thinking on things that is contrary to God's holiness given by Intitution. Conscience will make us uneasy as to what we are planning

to do, when Adam sinned his ability to distinguish good from evil increased, but the Function of Intitution was dead to God, also the ability to commute with God was dead even knowing good from evil, but could not be a Faithful Witness of God's righteousness of the Law by Adam's Knowledge of Right, and Wrong could not produce the Fruit of Righteousness of Faith. There must be a Conviction in Conscience before one can be saved, by Faith. Into God's grace, Conviction. In Conscience before Salvation is given. John 16:7-11. Heb. 9:14 Heb. 10:2 Intitution, and Conscience work together with institution to regenerate man Kind. Titus. 3:4-6, Believers then worship God with their quickened Spirit, Eph. 2:1-6 If there is a violation of our quickened Spirit our Conscience will convict us at the violation. Heb. 10:22. I Isaiah 59:19 Our Conscience testifies as being clean towards God Rom. 9:1, I John 3:20

We being born again must confess, and forsake all unrighteousness of self or Soul Life. Conscience never argues or reason Conscience discerns God's Will through Intitution, and condemns everything which is not according to God's Will. Conscience speaks for God only his will not Man's reasoning of the Soul. God requires us to walk by the revelation revealed by Intitution in Conscience. Conscience must bear witness of God's Will, Man's explanation of right, and wrong will not please God Man's reasoning is of the mind, the mind is subject to error, God is not the source of Man's reasoning, that belongs to earthly wisdom I Cor. 2:1-8, Man's good works – will not cover man Matt. 7:21-23, I Sam. 15:22.

For one to walk in the spirit one must obey Conscience, get rid of imaginations stop trying to reason the ways of God with the mind, by way of the spirit, the New Man the mind must be revealed to conform to God's Will as a Faithful and True witness. Conscience must be sensitive to God's Will and reject reasoning of the Soul, Acts 23:1, Acts 24:16, I John 3:20-22, 2 Tim. 1:3, I Cor. 1:12 Conscience must testify of God's Will within the Hidden Man of the Heart I Pet. 3:4. Rom. 11:6 Conscience is limited by the knowledge that it has received by Intitution, once we have this knowledge we are responsible to walk in that which we have received by the Spirit our Conscience bears witness to the knowing provided by God, with in the reborn Spirit then we can walk with God in total agreement Amos 3:3, 2 Cor 6:15-18.

Old creation Life is the Soul the Nature demonstrated is Sin, Carnal.

New-creation Life is the Spirit the Nature is Righteousness.

Walking according to the Soul as the Life Principal must be denied. Luke 9:23

Soul is Man's self must be renewed Rom. 12:1-3

We are judged by how much of the Soul Life is lost within us I 2 Cor. 13:5-7

Put on the New Man, because the New Man desires what God desires Eph. 4:22-24

The New Man apprehends the Things of God directly not by searching of the Mind, or other things the World is cut off from communication with God

As believers grow the Spiritual Senses are exercised is know good, and evil Heb. 5:11-14, I Pet. 2:1-2

Having a good Conscience does not mean we are perfect, yet but are living up to all that we have received in Intitution Phil 3:1-21 Acts 24:16, I John 3:20 a good Conscience assures us that so far as our knowledge goes we are perfect that is the immediate goal, but not the ultimate which is total deliverance I Cor. 1:3-10 special attention to verse 10, three steps to perfection. Our Conscience is our standard for God's Leading. We cannot allow man to mold our Conscience. My Conscience is directly responsible to God, in all regards. If we allow man to mold our Conscience we will fail God I John 2:20, 27 Fear of Man brings a snape or trick Prov. 29:25

3. Communion – Is a part of the New Spirit that communicates with God in worship praise, thanks giving, joy. Which is expressed in the falculity of the Soul's emotion John 4:24 the Soul falculity must serve the Spirit Zech 4:6

### Rom. 5:20-21, Rom. 5:17

No unsaved person can apply the Law of God with success, because Carnal Man is barred from carrying out the righteousness of the Law of God because of the curse put on

Adam and Adam's offsprings Gen. 3:24, after Adam disobeyed God he was not subjected to God's Law for righteousness Rom. 8:5-8. Rom. 3:19-22. Only in Christ Jesus are we accepted by God Rom. 8:2, Heb. 11:6 Jesus is our Faith, he provides the substance Rom. 5:1-2 Man in his best state without the Spirit of Christ is all Vanity Psalm 39:5 IS. 64:6, we must come to God by the Cross of Jesus Christ. Our sacrifice for Sin's Nature then our approach to God is accepted in Christ Jesus our Lord, then the Curse of the Law is removed from us. Gal. 3:13 the Law is the Power of Sin. In the Sin Nature, the Law is Holy, but what separates from the righteousness of the Law, once we are justified by Christ Jesus, we can do the righteousness of the Law by Faith of Jesus Christ our Lord.

Man Kind will only do what is predominant within, whether it's Sin or Righteousness regardless they both work by the Power of God I Cor 15:56 the only way to Peace is the death of the old Nature, then we are no longer bound by the Power of Sin, but now we live by the Faith of Jesus Christ, even. Though the Law is the Power of Sin, and righteousness, God does not impute sin, the sin nature is barred from serving God Rom. 4:6, 8 2 Or. 5:19 Jesus is our Saviour because he did not come to condemn Man Kind but to save us John. 3:16-21.

Rom. 5:20 tells us why man in his Sin Nature cannot please God. The Law of Moses only revealed to mankind of his Sinful Lawless Nature, man could not please God with his Sinful Nature when he tried to do right the Sin Nature barred him from fulfilling his desire the Sin Nature under the Curse of the Law got stronger, the law was the power Rom. 5:20, Rom. 7:12-25, the law could not go against the Sin Nature, and produce Righteousness of Faith, I Cor. 3:1-18, so as long as man tries to serve God with the Law of Moses he cannot please we need the Nature of Christ Jesus. Rom. 8:12-17 The Law of Moses can only produce the ways of the Sin Nature. If Christ is not our Life grace cannot abound.

1. Grace abounds in the Christ Nature

2. Sin abounds in the Sinful Nature but God is the Power of them both Is 45:5-7 we must come to the reality that God reveals in his Spirit to his Children Proverbs 16:4 God sets before us Death and Life Deut. 30:19-20, there is no other being causing us to do evil, we are people of choice, and every choice we make is already predestined by God every thought is predestined by God Ezekiel 11:5, 1 Chronicles 28:9 Nothing is hid from God PS 139:7-17 The Law of Moses is against Mankind the Law of Moses can only reveal the lawlessness of the Sin Nature, the Law of Faith is the only way to peace Gal. 3:19-24 the Sin Nature hinders the mind's desire to do right. Rom. 10:4, Rom. 7:25, John 8:28 we must be Taught of God.

## The Law of Sin and Death
### ROM. 8:2

The Scripture in Roman: Chapter eight verse two states that in Christ Jesus we are free from the Law of Sin, and Death.

The Law belongs to God himself, there is but one law, and that law is God. The one law is revealed in Man Kind, according to the Will of Man's choosing we are made to choose Life or Death. We can choose death or life based on what is set before us Deut. 30:19 We must remember that the Law is Holy, because God is holy, God created man to be a Tree of Life, a son unto him. As we look into the Scriptures we see the Law manifested in <u>Three</u> Parts within Man Kind, that was not God's intention the manifestation of God in Man Kind is meant to be righteousness, one with the Father's Holiness Lev. 11:45, but when Adam sinned he became another phase of the law which is Sin, and Death the First Part of God's Law in Man Kind is righteousness well pleasing to God in every way righteousness of the law within Adam which is called the Tree of Life, Trees in Scripture refers to Man Kind Adam was a Tree of Life, because of his righteousness within him, his Spirit was a Container for God's righteousness, which was the Life of Adam.

When Adam disobeyed God's commandment of God willfully he became a Tree of the Knowledge of Good, and Evil separated his spirit from righteousness to Sin Rom. 5:12, now being separated from God's righteousness within his Spirit. Adam could no longer communicate with God within his Spirit, which is the only way God will lead man king is within the Spirit of Man. God does not communicate with Man's Soul directly we receive direct guidance from God within our spirit, Gen. 2:7 Job 32:8, Prov. 20:27, we can only be led by God's Spirit of God within our Spirit. Rom. 8:14 when Adam sinned he lost access to God in Spirit, now the only way for Adam to communicate with God would be his Soul Falculties, his Will, Emotion, Intellect, the Soul Falculties cannot receive direct revelations from God the Soul can only received in his Spirit by the Spirit of God. The heart of Man is the Soul of Man look at what God said about the Heart or Soul of Man Jere. 17:9-10, I Cor. 2:9-16. We see that the Soul of Man is not fit to receive direct revelations from the Spirit of God, when Adam sinned he could only imagine. The ways of God in his Soul I Cor. 10:5-7. The Soul of Man walks by outward appearance not the inward witness of the Spirit of God.

After Adam brought death on all Man Kind, then entered the Law of Moses. The Law of Moses revealed man to himself to know what was in Man Kind by Adam's Transgression, the Sin Nature dominated Man Kind from Adam to the Time of the Law given by God to Moses to show man his ways was not pleasing to God, the law was not given to perfect Man Kind, but to show man his transgressions, true there were people at that time that feared God, and desired to live a righteous, but the Sin Nature stood in the way of God's righteousness mentally accenting to a Spiritual Truth. From God is not sufficient, we must have the Spirit reborn to be led by God Spirit. The Law of Moses could help Man Kind to keep man from totally destroying one another, that Law of Moses could not keep man in right standing with

God because of Adam's creation, John 8:44 Jesus speaking of Adam tells us about our First inheritance from Adam because of his Transgression. The Nature of Adam. The mind could know right from wrong to some extent he cannot performs the righteousness required by God. Rom. 7:19-25. Heb. 9:14-15, Heb. 9:24. Gal. 3:21-29

The Law of the Spirit of Life in Christ Jesus we have access to God's Grace Rom. 5:1-2, Matt. 5:17, now that Christ Jesus is our Life. We have access to God our Father not just our creator but our Father, we have the Incorruptible Seed the word God. (Christ Jesus) our life Gal. 4:6. Our new Spirit in the Image of Christ Jesus is now God's Tabernacle, he now walks within us, and talks with in us I Cor. 6:15-18, before Christ we were bound by the Sin Nature. The Curse of Adam kept us bound up in darkness Is. 61:1-3, when Jesus went to the Cross and the old way of entering into God's presence was done away with Matt. 27:50-53, Job. 19:25-27, John 11:25-26, Christ Jesus within us is our way to worship the Father in Spirit, and Truth, John. 4:24. There is no other way into the Presence of God. Jesus is the only way Acts 4:12, John 14:6. We see that God has given us a Free Will to choose Life or Death, God does not force us to serve him we have the First Adam, and the last Adam they both demonstrated the consequences of our choice. Adam demonstrated the Choice of Death. Jesus demonstrated the Life of Righteousness. Choose Jesus in him is Life.

## I in you and you in me

Jesus made a statement in the book of John Jesus said that he was in the father, and the Father in him, john 14:10, he was preparing his disciples for a new covenant by which his spirit that he had demonstrated among them for three, and a half years would also be in them once he had given himself a sacrifice for our sin nature Jesus went on to say that he would come to his disciples once the sacrifice was accepted by God our Father, john 14:11-14 he said that the disciples would have his name meaning nature he went on to say that the spirit of truth would come which is in his nature, Jesus is the spirit of truth in each born again person. When we receive Jesus to be our Lord, and Saviour we have the spirit of truth with in our spirit, in John 14:15-21 Jesus is telling his disciples how they would live the life that he purchased for them with his own blood. The question is how will this life be manifested with in man kind.

## He will send us a Comforter
## Which is the Holy Ghost

When the Comforter comes he will lead the new spirit with in man kind in all the truth that is with in the new spirit of man kind, in Christ we are the spirit of truth, but we need help, to lead us in the way we should walk being new creatures in Christ 2Cor.5:17, the Holy Ghost is here to lead us, and guide us In all of the truth with in us by

Jesus Christ our Lord john 16:13.Jesus being our example of how we are to walk in newness of spirit tells us that we are not to look to our own understanding of what God is doing or what he is like he by the Holy Ghost will lead us by his spirit John8:28 abiding in Christ we will know that we are walking in God's truth by yielding to the leading of the Holy Ghost, we must always remember with Christ Spirit with in us we have the spirit of truth the Holy Ghost is to help us walk in the new life giver by God our Father, John 16:13 tells us how this is done first remember even having the spirit of truth we do not walk apart from the leading of the Holy Ghost that is what he is telling us in the scripture, the sprit must follow the leading of the Holy Ghost, then the truth that is in us in Christ nature will be glorified, the scriptures says that the Holy Ghost will glorify Jesus meaning our nature will be manifested which is the image of Christ Jesus Eph.4:22-24.our responsibility is to stay humble with in our souls, walk by faith not by sight, renew the mind Rom.12:1-3.We must examine our selves to know if we are in the faith 2Cor.13:5-10. To know is to refuse to lean to our understanding according to sense observation we must follow the leading of the inner man the inner man is where the Holy Ghost leads us not sense observation, luke 17:20-21, we must know that we have Christ Spirit living with in us then we can rest in knowing that we are being led perfect by God's spirit with in,1john2:20,27 do not take on the philosophy of men Colossians 2:1-23, Gal.2;20, Gal.6:14. knowing these truths will keep us from walking in darkness of ignorance of truth we are free John 8:32, to worship God in spirit and truth John 8:24, knowing this is to be accepted by him Matt.7:15-23. This is the way the Lord has chosen for us. PRAISE GOD FOR HIS MERCY, AND COMPASSION, TO ALL THAT TRUST HIM.

Printed in the United States
by Baker & Taylor Publisher Services